Pooling Health Insurance Risks

Pooling Health Insurance Risks

Mark Pauly
and
Bradley Herring

The AEI Press

Publisher for the American Enterprise Institute
WASHINGTON, D.C.
1999

BOD 6745 - 4/2

ailable in the United States from the AEI Press, c/o Publisher Re-
irces Inc., 1224 Heil Quaker Blvd., P.O. Box 7001, La Vergne, TN
086-7001. To order, call 1-800-269-6267. Distributed outside the
ited States by arrangement with Eurospan, 3 Henrietta Street, London
C2E 8LU, England.

Library of Congress Cataloging-in-Publication Data

Pauly, Mark V., 1941–
    Pooling health insurance risks / Mark Pauly and Bradley Herring.
      p.   cm.
    Includes bibliographical references and index.
    ISBN 0-8447-4119-1 (cloth : alk. paper)
    ISBN 0-8447-4120-5 (paper : alk. paper)
    1. Insurance, Health—United States.   2. Insurance pools—United
States. I. Herring, Bradley. II. Title.
HG9396.P383   1999
368.38'2'00973—dc21   99-046267

1   3   5   7   9   10   8   6   4   2

The AEI Press
Publisher for the American Enterprise Institute
1150 17th Street, N.W., Washington, D.C. 20036

Printed in the United States of America

Contents

Acknowledgments

This research was supported by the Robert Wood Johnson Foundation's Program for Investigator Awards in Health Policy Research.

We are grateful for helpful comments from Jon Gabel, Bryan Dowd, and the participants in the Ninth Annual Health Economics Conference at Cornell University, especially Charles Phelps and Will Manning.

Rajiv Shah provided helpful research assistance for the work on the tax subsidy.

1

❖

Introduction

No one can be guaranteed a future of good health. There is always a risk of illnesses or injuries, events that are often and appropriately accompanied by high levels of spending on medical services. For this reason, all consumers face the risk of generating and receiving large medical bills. To convert such possibilities of large expenses into smaller and certain payments, risk-averse consumers seek and obtain insurance that covers some of the cost of medical care.

Purpose

Health insurance can help directly with the financial consequences of health risk and, by increasing access to care, make possible some alleviation of the threats to health. For both of these reasons, a majority of Americans who are not eligible for public insurance voluntarily arrange for insurance coverage for themselves and their dependents. How well do private insurance markets function to smooth or pool these expenses? Do some parts or types of insurance markets work better than others? Should steps be taken to improve market functioning, and might some actions, while helping to hold down medical-care spending or achieve greater equity, simultaneously threaten the appropriate pooling of risk?

This study investigates the extent of risk pooling in private health insurance markets in the United States. At present, such markets are subject to a hodgepodge of state and federal regulations, with rules, mandates, and subsidies ebbing and flowing at a moderately rapid rate. It is the present unsettled state of these markets that provides the policy motivation for questions about performance. This book addresses the question of how markets could perform by offering a combination of analysis based on the economic theory of competitive insurance markets and empirical evidence concerning the performance of markets from a period in the recent past when markets were less regulated and less changeable than they are now. We look primarily at data from the 1987 National Medical Expenditure Survey (NMES), a time period when those markets were subject to considerably less federal and state regulation than now exist. The study focuses specifically on the question of whether employment-based group insurance, furnished in various settings, is more effective as a mechanism to pool risk than is nongroup (individual) insurance.

Despite some significant erosion, the employment-based mechanism is currently by far the most common way of furnishing private health insurance to consumers in the United States. The performance of the employment-based market is increasingly criticized, from both the left and the right, as deficient and inadequate. This study will suggest ways to improve public policy and private behavior.

The policy trade-off is between group health insurance, provided through the employment setting, and nongroup health insurance, marketed and purchased in the same way as other consumer insurances, such as homeowner's or auto insurance. At present, public policy favors group insurance, providing it with a tax subsidy (to be discussed in chapter 5) in excess of $100 billion per year (Sheils and Hogan 1999).

On the one hand, group insurance based on employment does have several defects relative to individual insurance. It links insurance to the job, so that insurance often must be lost or altered when jobs are changed. Its amount and type are usually chosen, with at best limited variety, for all members of a group; some employees will not get what they want. On the other hand, group insurance does have some major virtues as well. One is a lower administrative cost, but the most frequently cited advantage justifying the tax subsidy is the greater extent of pooling believed to occur in group markets. It is this latter advantage that we will primarily consider in this study, although we will deal with the former as well.

We intend that our conceptual and empirical research will help in the evaluation of the trade-off between the advantages and the disadvantages of group relative to individual insurances. We do not suppose, however, that our results on relative performance can fully settle the decision, for any citizen or for society. That is because a decision depends not only on the facts about the extent of job mobility, worker preferences, subsidy-induced overpurchasing, lower administrative costs, and relative pooling; it depends also on how these characteristics are valued. It depends on how the undoubted inefficiency associated with some aspects of group insurance are weighted in one's value calculus relative to the efficiency and equity associated with low-cost administration and pooling. Nevertheless, unless people place an infinite value on pooling or efficiency, the information we provide in this study should affect some, and perhaps many, of those trying to make the trade-offs.

The theoretical insight that guides this study is as follows: if consumers value risk pooling, then competitive markets would be expected to develop ways to produce that pooling—perhaps not perfectly, but at least to a moderate extent. Conversely, market failures in insurance should have specific reasons that can be identified and measured. The empirical portion of the study uses data from the NMES to examine the relative extent of risk pooling across three different submarkets: large, employment-based group insurance; small-group insurance; and individual (nongroup) insurance. It finds that all three markets pool risk to some extent, and that the differences among the three markets are smaller than is usually thought. On the one hand, our analysis and that of others suggest that some risk characteristics lead to variations in wages paid to employees in insured groups. There is not as much risk pooling in large-employment groups as first appears. On the other hand, the individual (or nongroup) market appears to involve considerably more pooling than is conventionally believed. We also suggest, in a tentative fashion, that our analysis and that of others describe a market that is making trade-offs consistent with efficiency, except when subject to distortions from the regulatory and tax system. Although certain additional public policies could potentially help, the road to good performance may not be so hard to find.

Three Different Markets

Private health insurance in the United States is sold in three different markets with different economic structures (see Office of Technology

Assessment [1988] for an analysis of these markets). The smallest market is that for nongroup or individual health insurance, a market much like the setting in which almost all American consumers buy their fire, auto, theft, or life insurance. While some of this nongroup health insurance supplements group insurance (private or public), there is a portion of the population, estimated to be about 7 percent of those with private insurance, that obtains its primary health insurance in this setting. In contrast, group health insurance furnishes coverage for the majority of the population and is overwhelmingly based on employment-related groups. (This contrasts with life insurance, which is frequently provided through groups organized by professional, social, or business associations.) Practices and performance differ somewhat between small-group (defined for our purposes as twenty-five primary insureds or fewer) and all other group health insurance.

The main distinction among the three markets is well known and is quantitative: the fraction of premiums used to cover administrative costs and profits, the so-called loading factor, is lowest in large-group insurance, higher in small group insurance, and highest of all in nongroup insurance (Phelps 1997). Loading commonly accounts for less than 10 percent of total premiums in large groups, but it can account for as much as half of the premiums in nongroup, individual insurance. This administrative-cost variation would probably exist even if there were no variation in risk, although costs incurred to measure risk add a modest amount to the loading factor.

The other distinction is more directly linked to risk variation and is more speculative: when the firm bearing the risk is an outside insurer, not a self-insured employer, the insurance firm is least concerned with risk variation when covering a large group and most concerned in nongroup insurance. As we shall see, however, this concern does not necessarily translate into outcomes that buyers experience, precisely because sellers alone do not determine the terms of actual transactions; buyer must agree with seller on the premium to be paid, in insurance as in any other product.

The primary focus of this study will be on the existence and form of *differences* in the way risk is treated in these three different settings. Such a comparison is of value in itself, but it is also a relevant and meaningful way to hunt for the effects of differences in a variety of institutional arrangements—effects that may point the way toward improvement in a given arrangement. Of course, even if there were no differences across the three settings, one should not conclude that everything is perfect. Some problems in private-insurance arrangements affect all three markets equally. We will comment on some of these problems, but they are outside the explicit scope of this study.

Risk Sharing and Voluntary Markets

Although we will not expect to discover or to advocate perfection in risk pooling in this project, it is nevertheless desirable to define risk pooling and to specify what types of it are achievable or desirable.

Basic economics teaches that unregulated competitive markets will inevitably lead to prices for any purchased product that are equal or nearly so to the cost of producing or financing that product. When insureds vary in the expected cost of their health insurance benefits, even under a uniform, single-insurance policy, the tendency in competitive markets is for premiums to reflect those cost differences—for premiums to be based on "risk." Here risk is defined (tautologically) as a measure of expected insurance benefits. In such cases, insurance still very much pools risk, but the risk it pools is the risk of unexpected things: which individuals, among a set of apparently similar insureds, will actually get sick and use care. It is *not* the variation in loss probability, which is assumed to be already known.

The tendency for premiums to be based on risk occurs for two reasons. Most obviously, selling insurance at a premium that does not cover cost will reduce the insurer's profitability: high risks will therefore be charged premiums at least high enough for the insurer to cover their expected costs. From the insurer's viewpoint, however, charging high premiums to high risks is actually much less profitable than charging equally high premiums to low risks. But when there is competition, low-risk insurance buyers also drive insurers to cut their premiums to levels below average, since low-risk insureds will not patronize those insurers who try to earn high profits on their business. In effect, profit-seeking insurers combine with bargain-hunting, low-risk buyers of insurance to produce premiums in voluntary insurance markets that vary with risk.

For many observers of health insurance, such an outcome is thought to characterize unregulated health insurance markets, and to be undesirable. It is regarded as distributively unjust, because it does not give equal access or opportunity for insurance purchasing (Light 1992). When insurance premiums are based on currently observable differences in risk, critics feel that insurance is failing to perform its appropriate social function of spreading risks as widely as possible (Institute of Medicine 1993). Is this criticism valid?

The first point to note is that in all but the most exceptional cases, risk-rated insurance would still spread risk. If the premium a person is charged is based on that person's *expected* expenses, insurers will always have substantial uncertainty about what the *actual* expenses of the high-risk person will be, even for a person with high expected expenses. The lucky high-risk person's actual expenses could even be lower than those of an unlucky low-risk person, although this should not be true on average. The key point is that high-risk persons still gain utility from buying insurance at the risk-rated premium, compared with being uninsured, since they pay a certain premium rather than running the risk of an even higher expense.

Even nonpoor, risk-averse people with high-cost conditions, such as AIDS or cancer, face a wide range of possible expenses in a given year, and would still (in theory) prefer to pay a high fixed-dollar premium rather than risk the highest possible out-of-pocket expense. That is, even when risk is segmented it is virtually impossible to avoid a considerable amount of uncertainty, so that there should always be a market for insurance. Only those whose future expenses are known with certainty should rationally choose to go completely without insurance.

Another, more technical way to say the same thing is to note that deviating from risk rating does not allow any larger aggregate, average monetary gain than would risk rating. For instance, under community rating, what old people gain from community rating simply equals what young people lose, so there is no net improvement—just a transfer from one population group to another.

This discussion has two implications. First, it implies that there will still be a voluntary insurance market, even if insurers should perfectly risk-rate premiums; this practice would not destroy the market for insurance (and, as we will see, might even expand it for some buyers). Second, and more important, a policy decision to reject risk rating and to require some other insurance-financing mechanism could not obviously be justified by the notion that risk-averse people gain from insurance. Those gains can be reaped just as well by risk-rated premiums. Rather, as enunciated most clearly by the Shapiro report for the Institute of Medicine (IOM) (1993, 169), a decision to move away from risk rating is a *value* judgment—the value judgment that, for example, the young and healthy should have to subsidize the old and unhealthy.

Such value judgments are at the heart (and soul) of the social and political issue. Some people (most of the middle-aged IOM committee included) would agree with the kind of value judgment just posed. Some other people, however, surely would not—and they are not all young and healthy. Since this is the case, there is no principle (other than the tautological one that a social choice will actually be made that reflects the political power of groups with different interests) that will govern matters. Other than telling policymakers, "Do what you want to do," this is not a very satisfactory situation.

At least two different approaches, however, may allow the discussion to advance further. Even if a value judgment is selected that dictates that above-average risks *should* be subsidized by all others, one perspective notes that acceptance of that value judgment does not rule out risk rating. Rather, a superior alternative is to permit insurers to risk-rate and then to make (ideally, lump-sum) transfers to those high-risk insureds deemed worthy of a subsidy. One of us and others (Pauly et al. 1992) proposed such a scheme. We conjectured that society might not choose to subsidize all high health risks equally, but might prefer to give larger subsidies to low-income high risks and to provide low or no subsidies to wealthy high risks (no matter how old), or to those engaged in risk-increasing behavior. The principle of letting the market achieve a competitive outcome and then redistributing to achieve equity is a well-known one in welfare economics, and the specific decisions on who is judged to be deserving of a subsidy are social decisions.

The second approach is to find a rationale grounded in risk aversion for community rating or other deviations from single-period, pure risk rating. That rationale is well known, having been suggested by Kenneth Arrow (1963) thirty-six years ago: some degree of risk smoothing can be rationalized as "insurance with a longer time perspective." Specifically, risk rating on an annual basis exposes a person to the risk that, as a result of a medical condition that affects expenses for a period of longer than one year, the premium for health insurance may itself become a random variable. Another way to say the same thing is to note that there is no fundamental reason why insurance contracts must fix the premium for only a year. At least in principle, the premium could be fixed at age twenty-one for the next forty-four years and, since people are probably much more equal in risk that is based on their forecasted lifetime expenses when they are younger, greater equality in premiums could be achieved.

If this second approach were to be followed, it would call for limiting the variation in premiums with some but not all characteristics. Specifically, risk-related characteristics that were a matter of choice in the face of equal opportunities, and characteristics that are certain or given, once the person is identified, should not be smoothed in Arrow's efficiency-based explanation. Characteristics that are the subject of random variation, such as the onset of a chronic, high-cost condition, should not lead to proportional premium variation.

An example of a choice-related characteristic is location. Some areas have higher medical costs than others, for reasons related to input prices, past history, and quality variation, and yet insurers are usually not questioned if the "community" rate is higher in one community than another. Buyers could choose to live somewhere else. An example of a given or certain characteristic is age: given that I survive, there is no uncertainty attached to the prospect that I will be one year older on my next birthday, and hence there will be no efficiency gain on that account from sacrificing resources this year to have lower premiums next year.

But although such limited-efficiency arguments are part of a correct economic framework, they are not usually part of the social-insurance discussion. The "principle" that rules out experience rating is therefore usually established by postulate, not by argument. It is sometimes called the social-insurance principle, but in most countries other than the United States that principle means a proportional wage tax for compulsory insurance up to some limit, and not community rating for voluntary market insurance. The principle, in reality, is only negative counsel: premiums should *not* vary with risk. It does not tell us, however, what (if anything) premiums *should* vary with.

This study's goal, however, is not primarily one of evaluation. We argue only that in explicit or implicit evaluation, the community-rating model is not a uniquely acceptable benchmark. The main purpose of this study is descriptive: to pull together the evidence on how much and what kind of variation in net premiums for health insurance actually prevails in both the employment-based group-insurance market and the nongroup insurance market.

The Efficiency Conundrum

Some (though not all) risk rating can be regarded as not only unfair but also inefficient, in the precise economic sense that everyone in a risk-averse population could be made better off if insurance with a longer-term perspective were available. The conundrum of efficiency is this: if such insurance is indeed more efficient, what might prevent the market from offering it? For most other inefficiencies, such as monopoly or teenage unemployment, we know what the cause is—private conspiracy in the case of monopoly, government rules (the minimum wage law) in the case of teenage unemployment. But neither conspiracy nor regulation seems to present obvious impediments to the emergence of health insurance with guarantees against premium jumps attributable to risk variation. Indeed, such guarantees are the norm rather than the exception in term life and other insurances. What is the problem with health insurance that appears to thwart even a partial solution?

The question is even more puzzling because it appears that non-group health insurance (like its close cousin, term life insurance) *does* offer guaranteed renewability. Of course, what we should expect here is not literally guaranteed premiums; unlike life insurance, health insurance pays benefits in service terms, not in monetary terms, and overall price levels fluctuate. It should be possible, however, to guarantee that premiums would not change when individual risk changes, or would change only in rare circumstances.

It appears from David Cutler's work that some level of reduction in the variability of premiums can be obtained (for a price) in the small-group market. Cutler (1994) found that employers with stronger demands for stable premiums actually experienced stable premiums. But he did not look specifically at the effect of risk variation on premiums. His results suggest that in certain respects consumers have obtained greater de facto stability in their premiums than would be supposed based only on insurers' alleged rating practices. Alternatively, if there *is* premium fluctuation, it must not be so harmful as to provoke the emergence of institutions that could guard against it. The main conclusion, then, is that our evaluation of risk rating—even the kind that subjects people to apparently above-average premiums over time—should be tempered by the recognition that risk pooling may represent more than meets the eye. Furthermore, there may be factors more important than avoiding premiums that vary with risk.

Conclusion

How much risk pooling should there be? The answer, as to so many questions in economics, is "it all depends." The answer depends on what we take as our benchmark or definition of desirability, and on what we assume about other trade-offs. Below we organize these criteria for judgment in what we perceive to be a decreasing order of appeal. For the most part we use the efficiency criterion, as modified to incorporate a longer-term perspective, in our ranking.

1. *The most important gap in risk pooling is the incompleteness or absence of insurance coverage.* A person with complete but risk-rated insurance does face the risk of having the premium jump, should an illness occur that persists over multiple time periods. In virtually all cases, however, much larger threats will occur to lifetime wealth and access to care, even over the long run, if insurance fails to cover some big-ticket expenditure, or if the person lacks insurance altogether. In this sense, we would regard it as both less efficient and less equitable for a reasonably healthy young person to lack coverage against potentially enormous total medical care costs than for a middle-aged person with mild diabetes to pay a slightly elevated premium for insurance.

2. *The most important kind of risk to pool is the risk of chronic and costly conditions.* Risk-averse people want protection against unexpected fluctuations in their lifetime wealth, and risk rating that adjusts premiums over a shorter-term perspective may expose them to risk. Paradoxically, brief, sharp jumps in premiums for acute illnesses are less harmful than are permanent but smaller increases in premiums associated with a chronic illness. Of course, if premiums do not vary with risk but buyers are permitted to vary the amount of insurance they buy, adverse selection could ensue. Methods do exist to prevent this from happening—but they all require buyers as well as sellers voluntarily to take a longer-term perspective, something that may be difficult to do. In any case, the largest potential efficiency losses would be those that arise from risk rating based on future characteristics that are themselves uncertain.

3. *Failure to pool "risk" associated with age, gender, or location may not always be regarded as seriously undesirable on equity grounds.* The need to deal with this last category of risk factors is much more a matter of opinion, and that opinion in turn may be related to the correlation of these factors with income, wealth, or even life expectancy. For example, not everyone would agree that it is undesirable for middle-aged workers to pay higher insurance premiums than young workers pay, especially since income is related to age. Such transfers are matters of judgment about equity, and of relative political power. Be-

yond this, little more can be said other than that reasonable people may reasonably differ. In our later analysis, however, we will not regard variation in premiums with age or gender, or with location in high medical cost areas, as prima facie undesirable. But we will describe and document such variation.

2

✣

Conventional Views of Risk Pooling: What Do We Know and What Should We Expect?

We have two goals in this chapter. First, we want to present what we believe to be the current, generally accepted views of how the three different kinds of insurance markets behave, and the evidence in support of those views. Then we want to sketch out some preliminary conceptual reasons for questioning the views, reasons we will explore further in subsequent chapters.

What Do We Think We Know about Health Insurance Markets?

For most commentators, the way health insurance appears to be provided in many large firms comes close to the ideal, and is judged to be superior in terms of risk pooling to what allegedly happens in small-group and nongroup markets. (The lower administrative cost in large firms is surely an advantage.) Such firms typically self-insure, but their pools are so large that the average insurance benefit per unit is highly predictable. Almost all employees eligible for coverage take insurance, since a large share of the premium is withheld (pre-tax) from total compensation, regardless of whether the person elects coverage. Any employee premium share that does exist, in the spirit of what Uwe Reinhardt (1997) has termed "corporate socialism," is uniform within the plan, given the composition of the insured unit—for example, worker only, worker plus spouse, workers plus spouse and children, and so forth. (This socialism appears not to extend to basing employee contributions on ability to pay, however; the employee premium for a given policy is usually the same for an executive as for a clerical worker.) For example, Light (1992, 2504) asserts that in large-group insurance, high-risk "people were protected as employees of a group policy, because there was no risk rating within groups."

At the other extreme, it is alleged, insurance firms selling nongroup or individual insurance try very hard to avoid selling insurance to high risks, and to charge them very high premiums when they cannot avoid making a sale. That is, premiums increase with risk, at least proportionately, if not more strongly (just to be on the safe side). Anecdotes are bound to provide the bulk of evidence on this matter, since unusually high risks are by definition rare.

Small groups supposedly fall between these extremes. They might like to be card-carrying corporate socialists like their larger counterparts; they *try* to charge all employees the same employee premium. But in the absence of regulation, insurers will underwrite small groups containing high risks only at higher premiums. If the group contains fewer than ten members, individual workers may have their risk assessed, so that the total premium varies to some extent with the average risk in the group. Small groups, in this view, have problems when one of their workers is a high risk. An obvious problem is the potentially forfeited employer profit if premiums rise with the presence of a high risk, but it is also alleged that high risks may be dropped from or refused coverage.

To sum up: "Individuals (buying nongroup coverage) . . . may pay premiums that are significantly higher than the standard rate for the same coverage. Unlike employer-sponsored coverage for which the risk is spread over the entire group, (nongroup) carriers . . . determine premium price and eligibility on the basis of the risk indicated by each individual's demographic characteristics and health status" (Government Accounting Office 1996, 3–4). Light (1992, 2504) has codified these practices in what he calls the "inverse coverage" law: "The more people need coverage, the less likely they are to get it or the more they are likely to pay for it."

Within this pattern of risk assessment, administrative costs also matter. Administrative loading in premium quotations sometimes runs as high as half of total premiums for nongroup insurance, although more typically it is in the 30 to 40 percent range that characterizes other consumer insurance. Small-group insurance can still show 15 to 25 percent loads, especially in the smaller entities. In contrast, large groups can have explicit administrative costs of close to 5 percent of premiums, although some additional expense is usually associated with their benefits-department operation.

Those who want to "pool risks" more extensively, then, have two missions: to transform small groups into copies of the larger ones, complete with low loading and within-group community rating; and to avoid nongroup insurance as much as possible.

What Does the Conventional Wisdom Imply?

In broad outline, the preceding section describes how most analysts think about the current performance of U.S. insurance markets. Why do they think that way? What evidence do they use, and will that evidence be sufficient to support their conclusions?

We argue that, both for large-group insurance and nongroup insurance, the evidence customarily used to establish how they behave and what they do is insufficient. The conventional wisdom may be true, but that is not demonstrable by the data at hand.

Let us consider the "corporate socialism" view of large-group insurance. That view rests on two propositions. Proposition 1 is that *employee premiums do not vary with risk.* Proposition 2, the mirror image, is that *what insured persons in large employment-based groups pay for their insurance in ways other than through employee premiums also does not vary with risk.* At the outset, we must say that only on proposition 1 can easy and obvious empirical evidence be brought to bear. We can directly observe employee-paid premiums. To establish proposition 2, one would have to determine what the "other ways" of paying for insurance are, an issue not immediately obvious. Does the extra money come out of employer profits or employee wages? If the latter, is it withdrawn evenly or unevenly?

Employee-paid premiums are, of course, not literally uniform within a firm or group. They are larger for "insurance units" that include more people; there is an especially large jump when the family unit goes from one to two persons, but they sometimes reflect additional persons beyond a spouse. Moreover, to the extent that the employee premium is a fixed proportion of total premiums, it will vary with the total premium, and that premium in turn reflects the average risk in a group. Nevertheless, in the final analysis, employee premiums are unlikely to be strongly related to an individual employee's risk.

Having said that, however, one should also note that the premiums employees pay for a given level of coverage vary enormously across individuals in different firms, because different employers pay quite different fractions of the total premium. Far from being the uniform-for-everyone amount that would represent perfect pooling, employee premiums come close to being random variables. Employers currently set employee-paid premiums to provide price signals when employees choose among multiple options (Cutler and Zeckhauser 1997; Levy 1998). In the time period of our study, such options were much less common. The premium an employee paid directly for a given level of coverage in the United States in large insurance groups still varied substantially; this premium may not have varied with risk, but it varied. It is not obvious that such variation should be of less concern than variation across persons depending on age, gender, or total risk.

Of course, such variation in employee premiums might, according to economic theory, be offset to some extent by variations in money wages. The higher the employee premium, the higher the wage. Although strong theoretical and empirical evidence indicates approximately full incidence on wages on average (Pauly 1997), employee contributions may not be exactly offset every time, creating the potential for quite wide variation in the effects of coverage on the employed insured's net family income. The work of Royalty (1998) does show that wages are increased when employee premiums increase, but the offset is true only on average, and is far from consistent.

These last observations raise the other key issue in employment-based health insurance. Even if we know the per-worker employer-paid premium (paid to an outside insurer) for a given group, we do not know its incidence. And even if its incidence falls 100 percent on all workers in the form of lower wages, there may be much less risk pooling than meets the eye, since the incidence may not fall uniformly across workers. For example, if firms seek to hire or retain lower-risk workers, they may not be able to reduce their wages to pay for the cost of high risks if a substantial number of other firms are hiring only low-risk workers. Owners of firm-specific (less mobile) capital, rather than workers, may bear some or all of the cost of insurance for high-risk workers.

We cannot establish on theoretical grounds precisely what will happen to wages. We certainly can say that averaging of the employer-paid portion of the cost in even-dollar reductions of every employee's wages is far from a sure thing. Even if wages do not reflect risk-related costs, at a minimum there may be an element of randomness, or of variation for other reasons.

The Magic of Employment-based Group Insurance

The institution of employment-based group insurance does have one strong advantage over nongroup insurance. It can avoid some of the distortions associated with community rating, and at the same time average the cost of the insurance over all workers within a firm (Pauly et al. 1998). (Of course, saying that it *could* achieve this objective does not necessarily mean that employers *will* choose to do so.) The group can manipulate the employee-premium difference across different types of plans to allocate people at different risk levels across plans, while adjusting wages to even out the total cost. Here again, labor-market conditions may not permit every possible adjustment, but surely something can be done.

Imposed Exclusions and Chosen Limitations

While the premium for a given nominal insurance policy performs part of the function of risk pooling, another part of risk pooling deals with the extent of coverage. When the risk varies, the extent of coverage may vary, either because of insurer choices or buyer choices.

The most obvious and most common insurer reaction to high risk is the preexisting-condition exclusion, which can apply to both nongroup and group coverage. In contrast to risk rating, implementing the exclusion does not require the insurer to collect information on preexisting conditions. Rather, that information needs to be collected only when and if the person submits a large claim. In the time period we are studying, only about half of all employees had such clauses (Pauly 1997), and they usually expired after some time. Nevertheless, the existence of such schemes may mean that group insurance pools less than if all employees in the group were covered in the same fashion.

Access and Cost in Different Markets

In the most fundamental sense, the best kind of health insurance market would be one that made good insurance available to everyone at low cost. As already noted, risk rating (compared with community rating or uniform premiums) raises the cost of insurance to some and lowers it to others, but risk rating could in theory still offer premiums that everyone would be willing to pay. In contrast, arrangements associated with high insurance-administrative costs are bound to drive some people away from insurance. In what follows, therefore, we look at the evidence on the performance of each of the three market arrangements—nongroup, small-group, and large-group—in terms of the premiums buyers would pay. Although insurers appear sometimes to refuse insurance to some individual or group, we will look at such behavior as equivalent to proposing a very high premium—so high that the insurer knows no one will accept it.

The Nongroup Market

As already noted, it is generally believed that insurers in this market charge premiums based strongly on risk and often refuse to insure persons at very high risk for any reasonable premium. What is the evidence for this belief?

The traditional evidence is based on the observation that nongroup insurers usually "underwrite" all applicants (Congressional Research Service 1988; Merlis 1999). Underwriting refers to the insurer's review of an application and the process by which a premium offer or proposal is determined. In nongroup insurance, this decision is made for each separate applicant, based on that applicant's characteristics. In group insurance, by contrast, if an outside insurer is asked to bid, it will review the characteristics only of the group as a whole, not of individual members. Often large groups "self-insure," bearing all or virtually all the benefit expense themselves; they therefore risk the expected expenses for the group.

We should not overestimate, though, the importance of the distinction between individual and group underwriting in the late 1980s. A person with a very high-cost condition will be identified as such in the nongroup market, and we can be sure that an insurer bidding initially for the business of a group will want to know whether a similar person is included in the group—usually by asking how many such persons are in the group. After the first round of insurance coverage, the level of claims paid for the group will reflect the experience of its high-risk persons, so it will no longer be necessary to ask about the characteristics of the population. On rare occasions, however, the departure of an especially high-risk person or set of persons may be reported to the insurer. Reporting is rare, because the occasions of departure are rare.

Having determined that an applicant for nongroup insurance is substantially above average in terms of risk, we would expect the insurer to propose a relatively high premium. How "aggressively" insurers underwrite is to a considerable extent variable across insurers and even across insurance policies (Chollet and Kirk 1998). According to a survey of recent insurer practice, which is probably valid as well for the period of our data, insurers do "rate up" premiums when an applicant is judged to be high risk. Roughly speaking, the maximum amount that a standard premium would be rated up is about 200 percent (that is, three times the premium for a standard risk). In the late 1980s, evidence indicated that about 20 percent of applicants for nongroup insurance were classified as "substandard." Above that level, most insurers would simply refuse to cover, reasoning that someone willing to pay such a high premium must be an even worse risk than they estimate, and therefore likely to subject the insurer to adverse selection. (About 8 percent of applicants were refused coverage.) There are a few insurers who will still cover such high risks, but usually with limits on coverage and exclusion riders or limits for treatment of the conditions causing the high risk.

Most of the underwriting and rating practices that have been studied are those that apply to an applicant new to an insurance company. While insurers have sometimes changed the premiums of those insureds who have experienced changes in health status, this behavior is not common; in the nongroup market there is implicit if not explicit "guaranteed renewability" at premiums whose rate of increase is based only on the average growth in expenses. This behavior is now required by federal regulation, but it was actually quite common even when it was not required by regulation (Harrington and Niehaus 1999, 460–61), with more than three-quarters of nongroup policies in the late 1980s containing some type of guaranteed renewability. More frequently, the person who lets an individual insurance policy lapse because of failure to make all premium payments will find much stricter standards for reinstatement with the old insurance company, if the person seeks to resume coverage. New insurers will also take the information on risk into account to the extent that they have it. It would be very rare, however, for an insurer to drop coverage selectively for a continuing condition.

The Small-Group Market

Small groups experience insurer-underwriting behavior that is intermediate between that of the large group and of the nongroup market. Especially if the group is very small, information on the risks of individual employees or dependents may be requested by the issuer. Moreover, even for somewhat larger groups, a stronger attempt will be made by the insurer to collect information on the level of risk factors for employees in the aggregate. There is less of an insurer expectation of recovering any unusually large payments in one year through higher premiums or premium adjustments in subsequent years. Data on previous periods' claims may be requested from new applicants who were previously insured. More attention is also paid to the proportion of the group participating: if this falls below a certain level, coverage will not be offered.

Variation in Risk Pooling across Markets

The order of risk pooling, then, is this: large groups pool risk effectively; nongroup insurance charges premiums that vary proportionately with risk; and small-group markets are less stable. These descriptions apply to the average or typical practice in each of these markets.

Analysis of these markets has generally been driven by these descriptions. Such an approach, however, can be in serious error. One way to explain the error is to point out that these descriptions will characterize actual transactions only if buyers actually purchase from the insurer or in the setting in which the typical or average premium quotation is presented. Such an assumption is implausible if buyers seek to obtain the best deal (rather than the average deal) for themselves. These descriptions may outline the transactions that sellers want to engage in, but they will very inaccurately describe the transactions that actually occur.

Competitive Markets in Insurance with Risk Variation. In this section we first explore in more detail some intuitions behind this challenge to the conventional view, and then offer some informal theoretical arguments suggesting what is likely to occur. In its most fundamental sense, the possibility of a mistaken inference that arises from observing insurers' stated practices is similar to that in a *Peanuts* cartoon in which Lucy opens a lemonade stand with a sign advertising "Lemonade, $100." When Linus points out that there will be few customers at that price, Lucy responds archly: "I only need one." Up to that point, at least, selling or posted prices were not the same as transaction prices.

In a similar spirit, an insurance industry expert is quoted as authoritative when he says, "If I were a carrier in an unregulated insurance market, I would insure only healthy people, drop them when they got sick, and make a ton of money" (Lee and Rogal 1997, 5). But if healthy people know they are healthy, and insurers design an insurance product that appeals to them more than to less healthy people (for instance, an HMO with coverage of exercise equipment costs), and the insurance market is competitive, then the proposed recipe for high profits would not work—the sought-after transaction will not occur. Competition would force down the premium for the product that appeals to good risks, close to the expected costs for good risks. Even if high risks could be dropped (or induced to drop out), the premiums would not continue to be high enough to yield high profits. Guaranteed renewability would also stymie this eager insurer.

Hypothetically, of course, if one could propose to sell any insurance to anyone at any risk level for a sufficiently high premium and shed those exposures likely to incur costs, one could make big money. But this is an underwriter's pipe dream: either it will not be possible to identify and shed the high risks or, if it is possible, the premium to be collected for the insurance of low risks will be much lower. It is not necessarily regulation that constrains either Lucy or the greedy insurer; it is competition. This is not to say that insurers do not sometimes appear to be pursuing the logically unattainable but tempting goal of selling insurance to people who will not use it at all, or that there are no gullible buyers or temporary monopolies. It does mean that they will not succeed in the long run.

Slightly more formally, if we want to model behavior in this market, we have to take into account the desires and behaviors of insurers *and* customers. Customers will seek to pay low prices, relative to the benefits they expect to receive, even while insurers seek to charge them high prices. Below we will consider four hypotheses about buyer behavior that may affect the way actual premiums paid (not just premiums posted by one insurer) vary with expected expenses: differential search, adverse selection, guaranteed renewability, and the winner's curse.

Differential search effort. Nongroup insurance may plausibly be modeled as a search good, in which individuals obtain premium quotations from different insurers. There is some subjective cost to seeking additional premium proposals. Individuals provide some information to each insurer relevant to their risk level, and then decide whether to buy from that insurer at the premium quoted. The cost of searching an additional premium proposal may be assumed to be independent of risk, but the size of the expected gain from seeking another quote is likely to be higher the higher the risk, because the premium level will be higher. It then follows that, in the nongroup or small-group markets, higher risks will engage in more searches than lower risks and will finally be able to pay premiums closer to expected expenses than would be true for lower risks.

The markup of premiums over expected expense, commonly called the "loading," would therefore rise less than proportionately with premiums, because profits relative to premiums would be lower for higher risks. It is customary in insurance economics to assume that the explicit administrative costs (the "administrative loading") are proportional to expected expense. Sales commissions are usually proportional, and claims-payment costs rise with the number and size of claims paid. This assumption is not based on precise data, however, and it may well be that actual selling, billing, and claims-payment resource costs rise less than proportionately with risk. If so, the total loading (profits and administrative expense), and therefore premiums, may have a less than proportionate relationship to average claims.

Adverse selection. Higher risks may try to conceal information that would lead to higher premiums, and they may sometimes be successful in doing so. In theory, such asymmetry of information, in which insurance buyers know more about their risk levels than insurers can discover, could cause serious problems for the functioning of insurance markets. But if insurers can identify only *some* risk characteristics easily, and the proportion of unidentified high risks is not too large, and there are insurer-administrative costs (as Newhouse [1996] has suggested) or low risks display some inertia in switching insurers or cutting back coverage, then a widespread and functioning market can persist. Compared with a perfectly risk-rated market, the average premium per unit of insurance will be somewhat higher, and the amount or likelihood of insurance purchased by high risks will be somewhat lower. These effects on insurance quantities do represent inefficiency, but they are the direct consequence of a greater amount of risk pooling than would occur if insureds could perfectly discriminate. Indeed, this equilibrium is the same sort as would occur under mandatory community rating.

Does such modest adverse selection/risk pooling actually occur in nongroup markets? There is some evidence to suggest that it does. Browne (1992) and Browne and Doerpinghaus (1993) find suggestive evidence that there is indeed some adverse selection in the nongroup health insurance market (using the National Medical Expenditure Survey's predecessor, the 1977 National Medical Care Expenditure Survey), although the results are not completely conclusive. They find that in the nongroup market, low risks (who buy coverage) buy less coverage than they obtain in group markets. If one is willing to accept their assumption that purchases in group markets are made as if insurance were risk-rated, these results are consistent with some adverse selection in nongroup markets.

Guaranteed renewability. As already noted, a larger proportion of individual insurance contracts come with some form of guaranteed renewability. This guarantee is not ironclad. The most common form of guaranteed renewability allows an insured's premiums to be raised if they are raised for everyone in the same class of policies. Sometimes insurers have stopped selling one class of policies in order to raise premiums for them but not for new insureds. But this strategy is obviously one that will create a poor reputation for the insurer; new purchasers will surely worry that the same thing could happen to them.

Guaranteed renewability does lock the buyer into purchasing a particular policy from a particular insurer. This limit should induce more care in the initial choice and more attention to the insurer's reputation. There is little evidence about actual behavior in this market.

Winner's curse. Suppose all insurers have the same access to information about the risk level of a potential customer. Each insurer must then make an estimate of that customer's expected expenses in order to propose a premium. Different insurers will develop different estimates, based on their earlier experience, their subjective judgment, and the actual information they happen to obtain. It does appear that insurers are not uniform in their assessment of risk (Light 1992). Even if the expected expense averaged across insurers just equals the (very large sample) actual expected expense, there will be some insurers who will quote premiums based on lower estimates, because of the assumptions they make and the sample of data they obtain. These insurers will then attract a disproportionate share of customers. The insurers who win the business will inevitably have lower profits than the average; this phenomenon is called the "winner's curse." (Such a winner's curse may explain why insurers with a sufficiently large number of insureds to pool *all* risk persist in adding a "risk factor" [Congressional Research Service 1988] in developing premiums.) If the variation across insurers in estimates of expected expenses is larger the higher the risk level, this behavior will lead to the distribution of premiums actually paid becoming less variable than any single insurer's estimates of expected expenses.

Other explanations. These four explanations all lead to an outcome in which high-risk insurance premiums are marked up over expected expenses by a smaller percentage than low-risk premiums. The same outcome would occur in competitive (break-even) insurance markets if actual loading costs are not proportional to actuarially fair premiums. While the constant proportion assumption is usually made, and while claims-processing costs and agent commissions are probably proportional, total loading costs might not be. Even if actual loading costs were constant, however, the elasticity of premiums with respect to expected expenses would not fall much below unity.

Some Distinctions and Some Hypotheses. Many insurers in the nongroup and small-group markets do appear to *try* to tailor premiums (or acceptance of customers) to risk (Chollet and Kirk 1998). There is considerable variation in how aggressively they do so, however, and no study has yet looked at the relevant random sample of firms to document this variation. Perhaps there is a sufficiently large minority of firms behaving unaggressively to enable a high risk to find a reasonable premium. For this reason, the nongroup market may not in fact entail as much risk-rated transacting as would be supposed, based on what the average or typical insurer posts as premiums or asserts as underwriting policies. Implicitly, however, most of the previous discussion assumed that the customer had to obtain some insurance, somehow. It is clear that for a high risk there are potential alternatives to paying high premiums, even if they are uncertain from a longer-term perspective: either cut back on the amount of insurance coverage, or go entirely without. In this section we consider in more detail the critical question: What insurance-purchasing behavior would we expect as a function of risk?

To answer this question, we compare perfect risk rating, in which premiums are proportional to each person's risk, with perfect community rating, in which premiums per unit of coverage are uniform for everyone. We divide the problem into two parts. First, we assume that all insurance policies will have similar coverage, and ask about a person's decision to be insured or to be uninsured. Then we assume that the extent of coverage can be varied, and ask what happens.

If there were no moral hazard in insurance, if people incurred medical expenses only when they had medical need, then we could say that, as long as the loading percentage were below some threshold, the probability of being insured under perfect risk rating would be independent of risk. The intuitive reason is that even though high risks are charged higher premiums than low risks, the value of coverage to them is greater. If high-risk persons cannot afford high premiums, they can even less well afford high medical expenses; that is, they cannot afford to be uninsured. In contrast, community rating could well cause some low risks to decline coverage, because they would rationally rather bear the risk of paying out of pocket than pay a premium that is much above their expected expense.

Even if there were some moral hazard, the conclusions of the previous paragraph would hold for persons of moderate to high income: higher risks should not be less likely than lower risks to be insured in the nongroup insurance market. For lower-income persons, however, things may be different: without insurance, their levels of spending could be considerably lower than with insurance, because they would cut back on their use of care. In that case, then, we might expect low-income high risks to be less likely than low-income low risks to be insured under risk rating. Under community rating, the reverse would still be true: high risks would insure, but low risks would not, even if the premium were "affordable," since low risks would not want to pay a premium that is high relative to the benefits they expect to collect.

These propositions will be reinforced for low-income buyers if an alternative, subsidized source of care or insurance is available. If obtaining charity or bad-debt care is an option, it will appeal especially to lower-income higher risks, since their risk-rated premiums would generally be higher relative to the cost (if any) and quality of the "free care" option they might find attractive. As before, lower-income people may be more likely to decline coverage if insurance is risk-rated and they are high risks. In contrast, higher-income high-risk families can less afford to be uninsured, because they have more assets and better incomes to protect. (Interestingly, if community rating is combined with good availability of free care, it may also be true that low-income low risks will decline coverage or will purchase less coverage; we can be sure that the availability of charity care will crowd out private-insurance purchasing by low-income people, but we cannot be sure on a priori grounds whether the effect will vary by risk level.)

What about reductions in the extent of coverage? Such reductions can take either of two forms: across-the-board increases in deductibles and coinsurance, or the exclusion of coverage for certain preexisting conditions. Insurance coverage is least valuable when the loss is small or when the event is nearly certain. High risks might therefore voluntarily seek insurance with coverage excluding their preexisting conditions, rather than pay the risk-rated premium for such coverage under fully risk-rated insurance. Under community rating, in contrast, high risks will seek to cover virtually all expenses, no matter how trivial or how certain, and will reject exclusions. Low risks will seek larger out-of-pocket payments if they seek coverage at all, and they will be less likely to seek coverage for high-probability expenses such as preventive care.

Under risk rating, on theoretical grounds, there is no necessary reason why high risks would be more likely to prefer high deductibles and coinsurance than would low risks, given some level of loading (Ehrlich and Becker 1972). From a longer-term perspective, however, before the high-risk condition occurred, one would want to be protected against both the risk of higher premiums and the risk of higher out-of-pocket payments. Such exclusions may make sense in avoiding adverse selection when selling to new customers.

The conclusion, then, is that under risk rating, coverage might rationally be limited for treatments associated with higher-risk conditions that are virtually certain to occur. For people who do not expect to use charity care, neither the likelihood of any coverage nor the extent of coverage (as measured by the size of deductibles and coinsurance) should vary with risk. For low-income people, by contrast, high risks may be less likely to seek any coverage at all. These propositions will be important in our empirical analysis, since they imply a low likelihood of self-selection behavior among the nonpoor.

Group Insurance: A First Look

Except for variations related to family size, the explicit or "employee-paid" premium for employment-based group insurance is almost always uniform within the firm; it does not vary with age, gender, or the presence of chronic conditions. The conventional wisdom holds that because employee premiums do not vary with risk, the total cost of insurance to the employee does not vary with risk. This will be true, however, only if employee wages do not vary with risk.

Wages and Risk. Economic theory strongly predicts that in the aggregate, employee wages will be reduced in firms that pay more for insurance coverage; for example, the variation in the employee share has been shown to be offset by wages (Royalty 1998). Should we assume that such wage reductions fall in equal dollar amounts across all workers? Or perhaps money wages do vary in systematic or unsystematic ways, but those variations are unrelated to the expected benefits under the company's health plan.

This question of "individual incidence" is important. Our main data set is provided by the Agency for Health Care Policy and Research (AHCPR). For firms that self-insure in our data set, AHCPR makes the assumption of uniform incidence (except for individual versus family coverage). If individual wages are affected by the individual person's risk level, wholly or in part, not only will the AHCPR's imputation be incorrect, but it may also be quite inappropriate to view the employment group as pooling risk. Rather, by setting uniform but low employee premiums while varying wages inversely with risk, the employer may effectively be risk rating. The alternative—setting employee premiums that vary with risk—may raise the portion of the premium that is not shielded from taxation.

Family Coverage. One employee characteristic that can affect the total premium charged or posted is the selection of family rather than employee-only coverage. Nevertheless, it is generally believed that any increase in the employee premium for family coverage understates the difference in expected expenses. While there are some important risk-pooling issues in association with family coverage (including the use of an extended family to pool risk), we will not consider them at length in what follows.

Conclusion

To test whether the conventional views on risk pooling are correct, there are then at least three things to be examined:

1. the degree to which premiums actually paid (by consumer or employee) vary with risk in the three different settings
2. the degree to which the probability of being insured varies with risk in the three different settings
3. the degree to which wages vary with risk in small and large firms

In the following chapters, we provide empirical evidence on each of these issues.

3

❖

A Comparative Study of the Relationship between Risk and Insurance Premiums

Chapters 3 and 4 examine a rich and relevant data set to see what actually happens to high and low risks in largely unregulated health insurance markets, both employment-based group and nongroup. In this chapter we explore how strongly risk (of various types) is related to the premiums actually paid by those who buy insurance: issue one, as presented at the conclusion of the preceding chapter. Chapter 4 investigates issues two and three, the possible reactions to premiums paid—the decision of whether or not to buy insurance and possible adjustments in money wages in firms that provide group insurance.

The Data

The data used for this analysis come from the National Medical Expenditure Survey (NMES) and its Health Insurance Plans Survey (HIPS). NMES is a large-sample household survey collected by the Agency for Health Care Policy and Research (AHCPR) in 1987 and 1988, describing insurance coverage, premiums, expenditures, and a host of health indicators that prevailed in the subjects' households in 1987. Compared with the present situation, at that time few states had rules or regulations requiring various forms of community rating or open enrollment. (There was some regulation requiring guaranteed renewability.) Moreover, in contrast with current markets affected by the Health Insurance Protection and Access Act (HIPAA) of 1997, in 1987 there was virtually no federal regulation of indemnity insurance premiums or underwriting practices. In particular, during this period Section 89 of the Tax Reform Act of 1986 had not become effective, nor had the Americans with Disabilities Act of 1990. There were also only modest amounts of managed care in group insurance, and virtually no managed care in nongroup insurance. For these reasons these data, though now somewhat old, provide the best information we will ever have on how largely unregulated insurance markets will function.

Although the sample for the NMES was greater than 38,000 persons, the survey queried insurance coverage in detail only for a part of the sample. After excluding persons over age sixty-five and adjusting for other missing data and some informal editing, we selected a sample of 4,151 "insurance units" (individuals or families who buy insurance), comprising 8,010 persons. Three hundred eighty-six of these units were nongroup policies, and 760 of the remaining 3,765 employment-based group policies were obtained from firms with twenty-five or fewer employees. We also consider, where applicable, 1,625 units not already obtaining employment-based insurance. This sample will be adequate for most of our analysis, and considering that group policies were about twice as likely to have nonmissing premium data, it reflects the relative rarity of nongroup insurance in the United States at the time of the survey.

What Constitutes Evidence of Risk Rating?

As noted earlier, there is virtually unanimous agreement in the literature that risk rating is a common and important characteristic of individual (direct or nongroup) insurance. To some extent, this conclusion comes straight from an alleged fact about insurance markets; according to Blumberg and Nichols (1995, 2), "the basic fact underlying risk segmentation in health insurance markets is the highly skewed distribution of health expenditures." That is, since in any year only a minority of a population will have incurred substantially above-average medical expenses, insurers will try to avoid the high-risk individuals who incur these expenses, or to charge them high premiums. But this apparently simple and powerful evidence is not really conclusive.

Such a distribution of actual expenditures does not in itself necessarily imply risk variation or segmentation. In fact, a highly skewed distribution of losses, with some units suffering much larger losses than others, is necessary to ensure some utility gain from insurance. After all, if everyone experienced about the same losses, paying premiums would be virtually equivalent to paying the same losses out of pocket. The distribution of actual expenses could be highly skewed, but if every person had an equal though small chance of a large expense, premiums would be both moderate and uniform in competitive markets.

What Blumberg and Nichols meant, presumably, is not that the distribution of actual expenditures is skewed, but rather that the distribution of expected expenditures was uneven. The problem is that expected or predicted expenditures for any individuals are not objectively observed by them or anyone else. The distribution of actual realized expenses (which is observed) does not provide much information on the distribution of expected expenses. Analysts therefore resort to simulations or estimations of expected expenses, but such estimates are intrinsically less "factual" than data on what actually happened. These simulations usually do show considerable variation in expected expenses, but that variation is smaller than the variation in actual expenses.

Whatever the distribution of expected expenses an analyst or an insurer might construct, it is surprising that there is relatively little evidence on how or whether this distribution is transformed into a distribution of actual premiums. For instance, in an example developed by the Lewin firm (Bandian and Lewin 1995), the average expected expense was about $1,000 per year, but the lowest simulated premiums are at a level of about $300. Do we really believe that insurers will sell insurance to some buyers for one-third the average premium? Perhaps not; perhaps they are not so confident of their expected values and will seek a higher premium to play it safe. Even at the high end, some tempering may occur.

What Really Happens?

Data from NMES can illustrate these ideas. The distribution of "insurable" expenses for the 8,010 nonelderly individuals is shown in table 3–1, panel A. While the mean or average expense per person in 1987 dollars was $797, the median was only $137, reflecting the uneven

TABLE 3–1
KEY STATISTICS ON ACTUAL AND PREDICTED INSURABLE EXPENSES

A: Key Statistics on Actual Insurable Expenses

Coefficient of Variation = 377.80

Mean	$797
99th percentile	$12,811
95th percentile	$3,220
90th percentile	$1,549
75th percentile	$450
50th percentile	$137
25th percentile	$22
10th percentile	$0

B: Key Statistics on Predicted Individual Insurable Expenses: Linear Prediction Model, Using 1986 Conditions

Coefficient of Variation = 85.61

Mean	$822
99th percentile	$3,710
95th percentile	$2,263
90th percentile	$1,592
75th percentile	$991
50th percentile	$647
25th percentile	$402
10th percentile	$223

NOTE: Number of observations = 8,010. All amounts are in 1987 dollars. Only insured individuals under age sixty-five with no public assistance are included.
SOURCE: NMES data.

distribution of actual expenses. Five percent of the population had expenses in excess of $3,220, while more than 10 percent had zero insurable expenses.

Contrast this distribution with that shown in table 3–1, panel B, in which expenses are predicted using observable individual characteristics such as the presence of chronic conditions the year before, age, smoking, gender, and location. (The specification of the risk-prediction model used will be discussed in more detail below.) Compared with the data in table 3–1, panel A, the range of expenses is much smaller, although the mean is virtually identical. Predicted expense is smaller than actual expense for approximately the top 10 percent of the two distributions, but it is greater than actual expense for the remainder. Although the range is narrower than for actual expenses, if insurers nevertheless based their premiums on these data, they would charge some people more than others. The range of expected expenses (from the tenth to the ninety-fifth percentile) would be approximately ten to one, so there would still be a substantial variation in premiums if they were set proportional to expected expenses.

In reality, as we will show below, the distribution of actual premiums *paid* appears to vary much less than the distribution of expected expenses. For the present, however, the key point is that the skewed or uneven distribution of actual expenses tells us almost nothing about the variation in premiums that would be charged in an unregulated market. Just as the great majority of automobile drivers do not have accidents but are not offered virtually free insurance, those who buy health insurance but do not incur medical expenses will still have sizable premiums, while those who incur large expenses will pay premiums much lower than their actual expenses; such averaging is the purpose of insurance. In what follows, therefore, we will largely ignore the variation in actual expenses and concentrate instead on the variation in expected or predicted expenses.

One additional, important message can already be obtained from these data: at any time, risk rating affects premiums substantially only for a very small fraction, less than 10 percent, of the under-sixty-five population. Even if premiums followed risk exactly, the very highest risks and the very lowest risks would pay quite different premiums compared with community (uniform) rating, but there would be only a modest effect on premiums for the great bulk of the population; they would still pay premiums close to the average. Mathematically, after all, the proportion of the population with expected expenses much above average has to be small. As a percentage of the premium, the variation from, say, the bottom quartile to the top quartile is not negligible. But relative to average family incomes of about $37,000 in this period, the difference in premiums is not large. To be sure, risk-averse people would prefer *not* to run the small risk of becoming high risks and facing high premiums. But the cost of exposing them to such risk is not enormous, relative to other risks they face. There are worse things (such as being uninsured) than having to pay above-average health insurance premiums.

How Much Risk Pooling?

Before examining the details of the relationship of premiums paid to risk, we first present some summary statistics on the variation in the extent of risk pooling across different subgroups in the NMES data set.

Descriptive Statistics. We first divide the sample by type of "insurance opportunities" and by income. Insurance opportunities are divided into three types: those available to workers in large groups, those available to workers in small firms (two to twenty-five employees), and those available to other noninstitutionalized adults—the self-employed, workers in one-employee firms, or those who are not employees. Regarding income, we split these subsamples according to whether the total family income was below or above 300 percent of the 1987 poverty threshold (adjusting for family size), as defined by the U.S. Census Bureau.

The descriptive measure of premium variation we use is based on the coefficient of variation (CV) (standard deviation divided by the mean).[1] Since the variation in premiums, even within a group, may depend on the variation in risk, we present a *relative* variation measure, obtained by dividing the coefficient of variation of premiums by the coefficient of variation of actual total expenses. Dividing in this fashion adjusts for possible differences across the group in the true variability of expenses. If there were no risk pooling because there was no insurance at all, this ratio would be unity for every subsample.

There are two groupings within such populations whose experience might be relevant to measuring the extent of risk pooling: only the insured, on the one hand, or all persons, insured and uninsured, in the subpopulation on the other. For the insured, the variation in total payment depends on the extent and form of insurance coverage, the variation in the premium, given coverage, and the variation in out-of-pocket payments. For the uninsured, the variation in total payment is the actual variation in out-of-pocket expenses.

There are two definitional issues. The first one concerns what might be called the domain of variation. If all persons bought the same quantity of insurance, then the variation in premiums would inversely measure the relative extent of risk pooling. But some buy less insurance than others, and some are uninsured. We deal with this problem by providing three alternative measures: the variation in premiums per unit of coverage for those who buy coverage; the variation in premiums plus out-of-pocket expenses for those who buy coverage; and the variation in premiums plus out-of-pocket expenses for all potential insurance purchasers, including those who choose not to buy coverage and therefore pay for everything on an out-of-pocket basis.

The other issue concerns the measurement of premiums and quantities of insurance. We measure the quantity of insurance by using an actuarial index developed by AHCPR. That index is constructed by applying the policy's coverage provisions to a standardized distribution of expenses (in our case, that of all insured persons), calculating the average value of benefits, and converting that to an index. This index is a value between zero and one, representing the proportion of total covered expenses paid for by a given plan averaged over the standard population. This approach obviously ignores moral hazard effects, but it does appear to provide a robust measure of quantity; our analysis found that there is a strong correlation between the constructed index and levels of both deductibles and coinsurance, with a less strong relationship to upper limits that are rarely binding.

Defining the premium is no problem for people who obtain nongroup insurance; it is the premium they pay. For those who obtain employment-based group insurance, however, there is a question: Is the premium the employee-paid premium (if any), or is it some measure of the total premium, whether nominally paid by employer or employee? Economic theory holds that, in many circumstances, the incidence of the employer premium is on worker wages. But there are potentially important exceptions. If a small group is charged a high experience-rated premium per worker because of the presence of a high-risk employee and capital is relatively fixed, the wages of the other workers should not, in theory, be reduced because of this (Pauly 1997). It may, therefore, not be correct to attribute the full premium to workers. An even more serious problem, which we shall discuss in more detail in the next chapter, is that the incidence on wages is not necessarily an equal dollar amount per worker.

Nevertheless, for this descriptive analysis, we accepted AHCPR's assumptions about incidence. For firms that are not self-insured, the NMES's premium is the employer's response to the question "What was the 1987 annual premium for all coverage held by this person?" For firms that pay premiums to an outside insurer, the employer's (unknown) imputation determines incidence of this total group premium to a total individual premium across individuals. For firms that are self-insured, the NMES data define the total group premiums as benefits paid plus administrative expenses, and then arbitrarily distribute this full group premium to an individual total premium on a uniform per-worker basis; the cost is split between family and worker-only coverage, based on the full-sample rate relativity. This means that employees in self-insured groups with high premium costs will all be imputed high premiums. Because of uncertainty about incidence of the employer-paid premium, we therefore show two measures for the variation in group premiums: one using only the employee-premium amount (for which no imputation by the employer or by AHCPR would be necessary), and one using the employer-and-AHCPR-attributed premium.

Some interesting results, shown separately for policyholders insured as individuals or as families, emerge in table 3–2, panel A.[2] Among the insureds, the coefficient of variation of "explicitly paid premiums" (the employee-paid amount in the case of group insurance) is *lowest* for nongroup insurance. For group insurance, there is somewhat more variation in employee premiums for small-group insurance than for large-group insurance. The median paid premium for each of the three demographic sets is, of course, highest for the nongroup insurance.

More surprisingly, the relative coefficient of variation of imputed total premiums per unit of coverage for nongroup premiums for worker-only ("single") coverage is lower than that for both small- and large-group coverage. For family coverage, the relative variation is, by contrast, highest for the small sample of nongroup buyers. There are apparent sources of variation in group premiums, even when the employer contribution is averaged, which lead to variation in those premiums that is sometimes very close to that for nongroup insurance. Indeed, based on worker-only total-premium relative coefficients of variation (and assuming a normal distribution of premiums on standardizing actual expenses), calculations (not shown) indicate that the probability of having, say, a premium at least 50 percent greater than the median is 23.3 percent for the large groups, 20.4 percent for the small groups, and 21.6 percent for nongroup. (Results are quite similar when simply looking at the actual distribution of premiums for worker-only coverage: 21.4 percent for large groups, 19.0 percent for small groups, and 22.0 percent for nongroup.)

Table 3–2, panel B shows variation in premiums *plus* out-of-pocket payments for all potential insurance purchasers; this measure

TABLE 3–2
COEFFICIENT OF VARIATION RATIOS, RELATIVE TO COEFFICIENTS OF VARIATION OF ACTUAL EXPENSES

A: Coefficient of Variation Ratios, Relative to CVs of Actual Expenses: Insured Units Only

	Sample Size	Weighted Percentage	Relative Coefficient of Variation Ratios			
			Total premium	Premium divided by actuarial index	Employee-paid premium	Premium plus out-of-pocket spending
Single policies:						
Large group (26+)	1,563	36.3	0.220	0.227	0.692	0.220
Small group (2–25)	405	10.1	0.195	0.217	0.855	0.196
Nongroup	277	8.2	0.204	0.207	0.204	0.215
Family policies:						
Large group (26+)	1,442	33.3	0.155	0.161	0.647	0.175
Small group (2–25)	355	8.7	0.204	0.222	0.770	0.208
Nongroup	109	3.4	0.328	0.349	0.328	0.344

B: Coefficient of Variation Ratios, Relative to CVs of Actual Expenses: All Health Insurance Units, Insured and Uninsured Families

	Sample Size	Weighted Percentage	Relative Coefficient of Variation Ratio (total premiums plus out-of-pocket spending)		
			All	Low income	High income
Single-person Health Insurance Units:					
Large group (26 +)	1,084	24.1	0.260	0.278	0.249
Small Group (2–25)	729	14.5	0.303	0.333	0.270
Self-Employed	147	3.3	0.292	0.594	0.195
Not Employed Full-Time	631	11.5	0.361	0.393	0.506
Family Health Insurance Units:					
Member at large group (26 +)	1,363	30.2	0.243	0.230	0.241
Member at small group (2–25)	436	9.3	0.270	0.340	0.217
Member self-employed	174	4.4	0.359	0.454	0.311
No member employed full-time	119	2.6	0.540	0.579	0.470

SOURCE: 1987 NMES data.

in effect adjusts for the generosity of the insurance purchased (if any). Those employed full time by small or large firms were easy to classify. We split the potential buyers in the nongroup market into two subgroups: those working full time (the self-employed) and their dependents, and all others not employed. We know that the high administrative loading in nongroup markets generally discourages high levels of coverage there. Because of the greater exposure to unpooled, out-of-pocket expenses in the nongroup setting, the order of variation in total payment is generally what one might expect: the least variation among persons working for large firms, and the most variation among the less well insured self-employed and nonemployed. The one exception is for the single-unit self-employed.

We also separated these units by income levels. For most of the subgroups, the relative variation of premiums within low-income groups exceeds that of high-income groups, suggesting a negative relationship between income level and insurance coverage, which we explore later.

This analysis is necessarily suggestive rather than definitive, but it does show that nongroup insurance is *not* always associated with more variation in premiums or premiums plus out-of-pocket payments than is employment-based group coverage. It is the higher prevalence of uninsured individuals among potential purchasers in the nongroup market, and especially those with low income, that leads to greater variation there. And this is especially true for people who would buy individual-only coverage.

This phenomenon is probably not attributable to risk rating as much as to the relatively high overall loading for nongroup coverage. That is, it may well be that the more serious problem with nongroup insurance is not that premiums vary but rather that premiums are high for everyone. These high premiums in turn cause people at every risk level to cut back on coverage, and the effect may be larger for those with low incomes. The result is that more people in the nongroup market are exposed to variation in out-of-pocket payments.

The Relationship of Risk to Premiums. The previous analysis describes how total premiums vary across people who obtain insurance in different parts of the market. As already noted, there are reasons for this beyond variation in expected expense; they include variation in administrative cost, variation in shopping behavior by buyers, and variation in the degree of competition in the market. In this section we discuss the specific relationship of premiums to risk, based both on previous research and on our analysis of the NMES data.

Let *I* be the index of insurance coverage between zero and one, representing the proportion of expenses covered by insurance, and let *E(X)* be the expected expenses of people with a given set of risk characteristics. Expected benefits, *E(B)*, therefore are:

$$E(B) = I (E[X]). \tag{3-1}$$

If the administrative loading is a proportion, *a*, of expected benefits, premiums *P* would then be defined by:

$$P = (I+a)E(B). \tag{3-2}$$

Under perfect risk segmentation, equation 3–2 would hold for every subpopulation with a given set of characteristics. It then follows that, for a given value of *I*, the elasticity of *P* with respect to *E(X)* should be unity, since all relationships are multiplicative. It likewise follows that the elasticity of premium per unit of coverage, or *P/I*, with respect to *E(X)* should be unity. These are the propositions we seek to test using the NMES data.

There have been some other examinations of risk pooling with the NMES data. Browne (1992) examined the NMES data for non-group coverage and found evidence that lower risks—defined by self-reported health status—contributed more to insurer surplus (premium minus average expenses) than did people at other risk levels. While Browne did not quantify the relationship between risks and premiums, his results do suggest that the relationship may be less than proportional. Monheit et al. (1995/1996) examined the NMES data for group insurance and likewise found redistribution: the benefits minus premium tend to be negative for lower risks and positive for higher risks. Again, only a relationship with risk, not its magnitude, is presented. But their risk measures included characteristics that occurred in the sample year but would not have been known to the insurer beforehand, such as a heart attack that occurred in 1987. Their "redistribution" may therefore only reflect the fact that insurance pays more benefits to those who happened to get sick and fewer benefits to those who did not.

Our analysis is conducted in two steps. First we develop and test models to predict medical expenses. Then we examine the relationship between the expected or predicted expenses and premiums; as before, we examine this relationship separately for nongroup, small-group, and large-group insurance. We adopt this two-stage approach rather than regressing the premium directly on risk-related characteristics because we are interested in the magnitude of the relationship between expected expense and premium, as well as in rejecting the null hypothesis that premiums do not depend on risk.

Specifying a good model here likewise has two parts or aspects: it should predict expected expenses well, but then those expected expenses should predict premiums. This means that many variables in the data may do a good job of predicting expenses, but then those predicted expenses might be less strongly related to premiums than an alternative, more parsimonious model, using only variables known to the insurer, would be. We will at best be able to generate a noisy but unbiased estimate of the insurer's expectation of expenses. In another sense, of course, expected expenses can be looked on simply as a weighted index of risk factors, where the weights are the estimated contribution of those factors to average expense. Normatively, this view is the more relevant one.

Expected expenses. Expenses are all predicted at the individual level; expenses for families are then the sum of the expected expenses of each family member. This formula ignores the intra-family correlation that is bound to exist, but it would be too complex to develop a model for each different type of family structure. In any case, this issue will only affect the results for those who obtain family coverage.

We estimated a number of different expense-prediction models. Models are distinguished either by the variables used to predict expenses or by the functional form. We considered three different sets of explanatory variables. One set might be called the "certain" determinants of expense, because they themselves are not subject to random variation. These variables include age, gender, and location. The second set comprises "prior uncertain" variables—principally binary variables for the presence of chronic conditions that began before 1987 (the year of the survey), and for whether or not the person smokes.[3] These could be viewed as partly subject to random outside influences, such as the presence of disease or peer pressure. The third set includes health characteristics that were sure to take their value only in 1987: chronic conditions that occurred in that year, as well as self-reported health status and measures of disability or functional limitations. (Nineteen eighty-seven values of the latter two variables probably were correlated with their 1986 values; we consider this possibility in the analysis.)

We explored a number of different functional forms to predict expenses: a two-stage logarithmic model based on the RAND health insurance experiment (HIE) methodology (Manning et al. 1987), incorporating the Duan (1983) smearing transformation; a two-stage model that instead uses a square-root transformation of expenditures for those with nonzero expenditures (as suggested by Manning 1998); and a simple, linear model. Both Mullahy (1998) and Manning (1998) demonstrate the potential multiplicative bias resulting from the use of the logarithmic model. Further, Manning shows that the bias (if any) resulting from the square-root model will be additive, so that the use of the logged predicted expense as an independent variable in subsequent stages will be unbiased. By not dampening the tails of the distribution, the linear model does the best job of predicting those high expenditures for which risk rating would be most apparent. The square-root model also showed a good fit to the data. In the analysis that follows, we limit our discussion of expected expenses to those predicted using the square-root and linear-prediction models.

Regression results. The regressions using only the first set of "certain" demographic variables display a low adjusted R-squared but generally high levels of significance for the individual variables in the regression. For the linear model, adding the 1986 "uncertain" variables to the "certain" variables raised the adjusted R-squared from 2.7 percent to 4.9 percent. Finally, adding the contemporaneous variables explained 18.7 percent of the variance. (For the square root of conditional expenses, these adjusted R-squareds are 5.0 percent, 8.3 percent, and 22.8 percent, respectively.)

Table 3–3 provides examples of expense-prediction regressions using the 1986 uncertain variables for both the linear model and the two-part square-root model. As indicated there, a number (though not all) of the chronic-condition variables displayed coefficients that were statistically significant and large. These measures do help to predict higher medical expenses.

One variable that research has shown to be a good predictor of a period's spending, but that was not available in this data set, was the prior period's total expenditure. It is unclear, however, that insurers would know this variable for new customers, or that they could use it

TABLE 3–3

MEAN STATISTICS AND REGRESSION COEFFICIENT ESTIMATES FOR PREDICTED INSURABLE EXPENDITURES
FOR PRIVATELY INSURED, NONELDERLY INDIVIDUALS

Variable	Mean Value	Linear Expenses: OLS Coefficient	Any Positive Expenses: Probit Coefficient	Square Root of Positive Expenses: OLS Coefficient
Linear expenses/Intercept	797.13	373.4		
Any positive expenses/Intercept	0.783		0.458**	
Square root of positive expenses	21.99			13.142***
Actuarial index	0.825	−74.1	0.025	1.437
Plan is an HMO	0.146	−18.8	0.173***	0.001
Geographic price index	0.990	195.0	−0.094	3.505*
Male ages 0–4	0.028	164.2	1.044***	2.139
Male ages 5–9	0.037	112.2	0.410***	−0.860
Male ages 10–14	0.045	−108.1	0.250***	−2.555
Male ages 15–19	0.034	46.1	0.284***	1.268
Male ages 20–24	0.038	22.4	−0.083	0.112
Male ages 25–29	0.051			
Male ages 30–34	0.052	138.5	0.048	2.557
Male ages 35–39	0.052	−85.8	0.114	0.071
Male ages 40–44	0.043	−154.9	0.178**	−1.508
Male ages 45–49	0.033	938.5***	0.192**	7.626***

Male ages 50–54	0.026	163.2	−0.022	3.987*
Male ages 55–59	0.025	496.4**	0.346***	5.941***
Male ages 60–64	0.018	2,288.9***	0.513***	13.978***
Female ages 0–4	0.029	218.5	0.965***	1.407
Female ages 5–9	0.035	−187.7	0.434***	−4.791***
Female ages 10–14	0.036	−14.2	0.279***	−2.431
Female ages 15–19	0.032	451.7**	0.331***	4.619**
Female ages 20–24	0.042	328.8*	0.670***	5.812***
Female ages 25–29	0.056	307.8*	0.770***	5.746***
Female ages 30–34	0.062	561.5***	0.784***	7.974***
Female ages 35–39	0.055	279.9	0.702***	4.825***
Female ages 40–44	0.050	317.4*	0.603***	5.071***
Female ages 45–49	0.031	240.3	0.759***	3.695**
Female ages 50–54	0.035	472.0**	0.702***	7.237***
Female ages 55–59	0.030	337.5	0.444***	6.037***
Female ages 60–64	0.023	243.8	0.725***	4.175**
Stroke before 1987	0.006	−60.9	0.165	6.052*
Cancer before 1987	0.022	792.3***	0.419***	6.805***
Heart attack before 1987	0.012	267.2	−0.086	3.594
Gall bladder disease before 1987	0.023	689.9***	0.269**	5.283**
High blood pressure before 1987	0.128	491.5***	0.330***	3.728***
Arteriosclerosis before 1987	0.007	759.8**	0.317	−1.989
Rheumatism before 1987	0.015	565.9**	−0.068	1.057
Emphysema before 1987	0.008	457.8	0.018	8.401***

(Table continues)

TABLE 3–3 (continued)

Variable	Mean Value	Linear Expenses: OLS Coefficient	Any Positive Expenses: Probit Coefficient	Square Root of Positive Expenses: OLS Coefficient
Arthritis before 1987	0.092	422.4***	0.428***	5.376***
Diabetes before 1987	0.022	841.7***	0.414***	8.638***
Heart disease before 1987	0.020	1,127.7***	0.725***	10.506***
Epilepsy	0.005	24.9	0.687**	2.949
Cerebral palsy	0.001	2,668.1**	5.335	14.049
Autism/Mental retardation	0.001	1,318.7	0.027	17.889***
Have smoked over 100 cigarettes	0.351	52.1	0.008	0.582
Nonwhite	0.209	−86.3	−0.401***	−1.093*
New England—Rural	0.004	1,701.6***	−0.275	9.475**
New England—MSA	0.040	−342.9**	0.036	−2.817**
Mid-Atlantic—Rural	0.025	21.2	−0.149	1.274
Mid-Atlantic—MSA	0.128			
East North Central—Rural	0.041	−274.2*	−0.115	−1.353
East North Central—MSA	0.138	−79.6	−0.001	−0.140
West North Central—Rural	0.042	−295.2*	0.183**	−3.037**
West North Central—MSA	0.037	−40.1	−0.044	−0.113
South Atlantic—Rural	0.088	−191.9	−0.139*	−1.643
South Atlantic—MSA	0.124	−34.6	0.000	0.868

East South Central—Rural	0.023	−257.7	−0.034	−0.709
East South Central—MSA	0.041	−133.6	−0.130	−0.027
West South Central—Rural	0.022	−321.1	−0.109	−1.251
West South Central—MSA	0.061	−379.9***	−0.158**	−3.178**
Mountain—Rural	0.024	−157.6	0.108	−1.265
Mountain—MSA	0.042	212.7	−0.051	0.921
Pacific—Rural	0.010	−367.4	0.129	−4.600*
Pacific—MSA	0.110	−167.8	0.046	−0.598
Number of observations[a]	8,010	10,025	10,025	7,821
R-square		0.0547		0.0897
Adjusted R-square		0.0489		0.0827
Log likelihood			−4,841.75	

***Significant at 0.01 or better.

**Significant at between 0.01 and 0.05.

*Significant at between 0.05 and 0.10.

a. We have a sample size of 10,025 privately insured, nonelderly individuals (receiving no public assistance) with complete data for actual medical expenditures, insurance policy information, and health status. This is diminished to our working sample of 8,010 individuals (comprising 4,151 insurance units) through both incomplete health status data for other dependents within an insurance unit and missing data for the number of employees at firms through which employment-based insurance is obtained. We use the full sample for predicting medical expenses, however, both to increase the estimation power and to reduce the possibility that we are "overfitting" our model.

NOTE: OLS = ordinary least squares. MSA = metropolitan statistical area.

SOURCE: 1987 NMES data.

for continuing customers. Insurers do ask new buyers about prior medical services (though not about the dollar amount of spending); their ability to verify this information at reasonable cost is not great. Of course, insurers would know the value of this variable for continuing customers, but (in the absence of data other insurers could verify) it is not clear why they would charge lower premiums to those whom they knew to have low prior-period expenses, since other insurers do not have the same information. An equilibrium does exist in such models (Kunreuther and Pauly 1985), but it is one in which premiums are uniform and in excess of expected expenses. For all these reasons, we do not think the absence of prior-period spending measures, however helpful they may be for researchers who wish to construct expense-prediction models or normative risk-adjustment models, will adversely affect our ability to explain variation in premiums with nontransitory risk.

Insurance premiums. We seek to estimate a simple model of premium determination. The dependent variable is the (log of) premium divided by the actuarial index, and the principal independent variable is the (log of) predicted expenses. Because the sample size is small, we combine family and individual coverage for nongroup insurance, adding a binary variable for family coverage. We examine family and individual coverage in groups both separately and combined. (In the data sets that pool group and nongroup coverage, a binary variable for employer-provided coverage is also added.) Results are shown based on the three alternative sets of predictor variables and two different specifications of the prediction regression.

Premium elasticities—that is, the ordinary least squares (OLS) coefficient on log predicted expense—are shown in table 3–4. For nongroup insurance, there is a clear and consistent pattern: elasticities are highest (at 0.30 and 0.44 for the linear and square-root specifications, respectively) when only the "certain" demographic variables are used, despite their quite low power to predict individual expenses. When the prior period's chronic conditions are added, the elasticity falls (as the range of expected expenses widens) to 0.17 and 0.30 for the two specifications. Finally, adding the 1987 variables causes the elasticity and the fit of the premium regression to decline still further.[4]

The main message here is important: premiums in the nongroup market definitely do not display the unitary elasticity consistent with perfectly risk-rated premiums. The elasticities are all well below

TABLE 3–4

ELASTICITY OF PREMIUM/INDEX WITH RESPECT TO EXPECTED EXPENSES

| | | Elasticity | | | | | |
| | | Linear OLS Model | | | Two-Part Square-Root Model | | |
Sample	N	Certain	Before 1987	1987	Certain	Before 1987	1987
All	4,151	0.07***	0.02*	0.02***	0.05*	0.03	0.04**
Individual	2,245	0.04	0.01	0.02**	0.00	0.00	0.04*
Family	1,906	0.12***	0.05**	0.03***	0.12***	0.07**	0.03*
Large group	3,005	0.03*	0.00	0.01**	−0.01	−0.02	0.01
Individual	1,563	−0.02	−0.02	0.01	−0.10**	−0.08**	−0.01
Family	1,442	0.11***	0.05***	0.03**	0.09**	0.05	0.03
Small group	760	0.04	0.00	0.01	0.05	0.02	0.04
Individual	405	−0.02	−0.03	0.00	−0.06	−0.03	0.03
Family	355	0.15*	0.05	0.04	0.20*	0.11	0.06
Nongroup[a]	386	0.30***	0.17***	0.08***	0.44***	0.30***	0.18***

***Significant at 0.01 or better.
**Significant at between 0.01 and 0.05
*Significant at between 0.05 and 0.10.

a. Subsamples for individual and family policies within the Nongroup sample are too small for separate analysis.

SOURCE: 1987 NMES data.

47

unity. A typical person in a percentile of the distribution of expected expenses whose risk level is twice the average will pay much less than twice the premium. Of course, because of other sources of variation, *some* high risks will pay premiums twice as high or more, but others at the same risk level will pay much lower premiums.

Further analysis provides additional and confirming detail: to the extent that premiums in the nongroup market vary with risk, they vary only with the risk variation associated with the demographic variables. To perform this analysis, we construct a measure of the "uncertain" risk by calculating the value of the predicted expense, including the "uncertain" variables, divided by the predicted expense, using only the "certain" variables. Such a ratio is centered on one and will be larger for those with more chronic conditions. (Note that we construct both prior-period uncertain ratios and contemporaneous uncertain ratios.) Nevertheless, regressing the (log of) premium divided by the index on either this uncertain risk measure alone or both the ratio and the (log of) certain expenses found this ratio to be statistically insignificant; the magnitude of the elasticity for certain expenses in the latter regression did not change substantially.

That is, holding constant the expense predicted by the certain variables, the variables representing the presence or absence of chronic conditions in prior periods (despite their significance in the expense regressions) do not help at all to predict premiums. Given their age, location, and gender, people with chronic conditions do not systematically pay higher nongroup premiums than do those without them.

Group-insurance premiums, calculated as described earlier, also showed some relationship to risk. For family premiums, there was a relationship with risk in both small and large groups, with elasticities that were statistically significant and in the 0.09 to 0.20 range. These relationships, as in the case of nongroup insurance, are almost entirely determined by the certain or demographic variables. Note, however, that the only expense-prediction variable describing a characteristic also shared with other workers in the group is location; all the other variables reflect only the values for the sampled individual, not for all members of his or her group. Of course, each individual is a random draw from the group, so there should be a tendency for the sampled individuals to reflect the most common or predominant values in their group.

We explored the possibility that the effect of demographic characteristics on group premiums might also be attributable to family size or composition. The method used by the Agency for Health Care Policy and Research for estimating family premiums for self-insured firms will generate the same value for everyone in a firm with family coverage, regardless of family size, but some outside insurers do adjust their family premiums for family composition. We found, however, that controlling for family size or composition did not change the estimated elasticity.

In contrast to the family coverage results, we found no statistically significant relationship between risk and the estimated premiums for workers who elected worker-only group coverage. For this set of insurance purchasers, premiums are truly independent of risk.

Further Tests. Viewed as measures of expected benefits, even perfectly risk-rated premiums are, in an important sense, variables measured with error. Insurers may try to guess what benefits a customer will claim, but they would be fortunate to guess correctly on average. As already noted, the errors-in-variables problem is compounded in any study in which the analyst does not know the expected expense value the insurer was using. If, as is likely, we are using imperfect estimates of what insurers believed the expected expenses to be, the elasticities of premiums with respect to our estimated expected expense could be biased downward, as compared with what we would presumably find if we knew exactly what the insurers had estimated. Of course, we cannot distinguish such errors in measurement from behavior in insurance markets that results in insurers' not charging premiums reflecting expected expenses (or, at least, the expected expense derived by the most skilled insurer). Still, even if our estimates are biased downward, our failure to find that people with persistent chronic conditions pay anything more for their insurance is suggestive of more than just mismeasurement. The NMES measures of chronic conditions definitely predict expense strongly. They should therefore predict premiums, if premiums are experience-rated.

A way of dealing with this problem of imperfect measurement is provided by noting that the errors-in-variables bias occurs when a variable measured with error is an explanatory variable. If, instead, it is the dependent variable, errors may cause the R-squared to be low, but the coefficient estimate should not be biased (Wonnacott and Wonnacott 1979). To explore this possibility, we also used both actual expenses and expected expenses as the *dependent* variables. The explanatory variables are the premium, which presumably is measured accurately, and the coverage index. In this case, however, the results (not shown) are very similar to those already discussed. Elasticities are virtually the same as before, at around 0.2, regardless of the dependent variable. That is, people who pay twice the premium for a given level of insurance coverage have, on average, only about 20 percent higher expected expenses. Premiums do vary, but largely for reasons other than variation in risk.

The overarching message from these data is that nongroup premiums do vary with risk, but not nearly as strongly as would be consistent with vigorous risk rating. Perhaps more important, they do not vary at all with risk as measured by chronic conditions and the other "uncertain" variations in the expense-prediction model. This is not to deny that some people pay very high premiums for their coverage, and that some of the people who do so are high risks. Apparently, however, many high risks do not pay higher-than-average nongroup premiums. (We explore later possible reasons for this.)

There are additional reasons, however, why premiums may be high, but they are unrelated to risk; the primary explanation is the inefficient shopping behavior of insureds. This explanation might imply, not surprisingly, that markets are not perfectly competitive if not risk-rated. Another explanation is that insurers are willing to ignore the presence of chronic conditions among their longtime customers, just as the theory of efficient insurance pricing would predict. That is, either explicitly or implicitly, they renew policies at premiums that do not jump after the onset of a chronic condition. Unfortunately, there was an insufficient number of new insurance purchasers of nongroup insurance in the NMES sample to test the hypothesis that risk rating is limited to new buyers.

Sources of Bias. While these results are striking, they may be subject to bias. One source of bias is the possibility that high risks in the nongroup market responded to the high premiums by dropping coverage entirely and, conversely, that the low risks sought coverage eagerly because their premiums are low. (Note that this is exactly the opposite behavior of what would have occurred under adverse selection.) The resulting effect could be to drop many of the high risks from the sample of purchasers, thus compressing the range of observations. We show in the next chapter that this kind of self-selection behavior generally did not occur.

The other possible cause of bias is that high risks might selectively drop coverage for some conditions in order to obtain insurance at lower premiums. The theory of insurance purchasing could make such behavior rational. If it is virtually certain that a person with diabetes, say, will need an annual eye examination, it is more rational for such a person to choose a risk-rated insurance that does not cover such a service but charges a premium lower by the amount of savings, rather than to select a risk-rated insurance that marks up the premium by the cost of the eye exam *plus* loading. In addition, higher risks may choose policies with higher levels of cost sharing across the board under risk rating, even though this behavior is not necessarily what would happen under rational insurance purchasing. Browne (1992) has in fact investigated this question with the 1977 NMES data, and found results that point in the direction of adverse selection: high risks buy more coverage, not less. Nevertheless, since we control for the level of coverage in the premium regressions, our elasticity estimates will not be biased on this account as long as the measure of coverage is accurate.

In chapter 4 we examine the first source of bias. Although we discuss the results there, it is sufficient to note here that the amount of bias-producing behavior detected for the bulk of the population is not large and is not very strongly related to the "unpredictable" risk factors. Therefore it appears unlikely that there is important self-selection bias in the results just presented. For this reason, we do not further adjust the estimates for selection bias, since doing so can often add error as well as correct it, especially when (as in the case of these data) there is no obvious, strong set of identifying variables for the coverage decisions.

For the second source of bias, there are actually two issues. If exclusion of preexisting conditions occurs but is imperfect, the proportion of expenses covered by insurance will decline as risk rises, but there can still be substantial pooling of the risk associated with the nonexcluded conditions. A simple test of the latter proposition is to compare actual benefits and expenses of high-risk people (relative to the average) to the premiums they paid (also relative to the average).

Table 3–5 compares average actual expenses, actual benefits, actual premiums, and expected expenses for two subsets of the population of individuals with nongroup coverage: those in the top 10 percent of the distribution of expected expenses (high risks) and those with expected expenses below the median of expected expenses

TABLE 3–5

EXPENSES IN NONGROUP INDIVIDUAL COVERAGE, BY RISK

	All Individuals (dollars)	Bottom 50 Percent of Expected Expense[a] (dollars)	Top 10 Percent of Expected Expense (dollars)
Actual expenses	1,020	373	4,021
Actual benefits	544	187	2,054
Premiums	945	825	1,150
Expected expenses	1,214	555	3,504

a. Predicted expense columns use linear OLS model with both "certain" and "before 1987" variables.
NOTE: Number of observations = 277.
SOURCE: 1987 NMES data.

("below-average" risks). Actual average expenses in the high-risk group, at $4,021, were about eleven times greater than actual expenses of $373 for the below-average risk group. Actual average benefits were similarly eleven times higher in the high-risk group. In stark contrast, average premiums in the high-risk group, at $1,150, were only 39 percent greater than those in the below-average risk group. Not only do premiums vary much, much less than insurance benefits or risk, but the proportion of expenses covered by benefits is virtually identical (50 percent for low risks and 51 percent for high risks).

There is a similar pattern (not shown) if we isolate the variation in expenses and benefits attributable to chronic conditions, that is, by the uncertain risk ratio: premiums barely vary even as expenses and benefits range substantially. Benefits as a percentage of expenses do fall slightly (from 51 percent to 43 percent) for the high-risk group relative to the other group.

Choosing Insurance

One message that comes clearly through these data is that there is no rigid link between risk and premiums, either in the nongroup market or in any of the group markets. In the case of small groups, David Cutler (1994) had obtained a similar conclusion. He finds that some buyers do indeed purchase insurance in which their premiums may fall the next year if they have good experience and rise (potentially substantially) if they have bad experience. But many buyers apparently choose to limit this kind of risk. He concludes that insurers are willing to supply the function of "tempering" or modifying the relationship between single-period risk levels and premiums for those periods. Explicitly or implicitly, people can buy insurance with a longer-term perspective, and some do.

Since the abstract theory of multiperiod insurance (Pauly, Kunreuther, and Hirth 1995; Cochrane 1995) shows that such arrangements are possible and potentially stable, and since there are potential gains in well-being for risk-averse people from buying such additional "coverage," this result is not surprising. It illustrates the general economic proposition that markets will emerge to facilitate gains from trade (Pauly, Kunreuther, and Nickel 1998). But the data also clearly show that this is not protection against all variation in premiums with risk: there definitely is not complete pooling in the nongroup market or in the group market.

4

❧

The Effect of Risk on Insurance Purchasing and Wages

Higher-risk people may respond to high premiums in the nongroup market by purchasing coverage less frequently than lower risks. Higher-risk people who are employed at small or large firms may also be less likely than low risks to obtain insurance coverage—although whether they are not being offered coverage, or are being offered but are declining it, is not clear.

In this chapter, we look at these issues of coverage with the National Medical Expenditure (NMES) data and try to determine when (if at all) high risk discourages people from obtaining coverage. Our main question is not whether higher risks somehow have a lower likelihood of being insured than have low risks; rather, it is whether any variation in coverage with risk is more *pronounced* in the nongroup market than in the group markets. Of course, if we find no relationship in any of the three markets, there can be no difference. As before, we will not only be looking at the effects of risk levels overall, but also distinguishing "certain" risk variation from "uncertain" risk variation.

Another important kind of behavior that could affect the results in the previous chapter concerns whether the "employer's share" of the premium in group markets is not offset through the uniform reduction in wages implicitly assumed in all other studies. We therefore also want to see whether wages will be differentially reduced for high-risk units relative to low-risk units, compared with wages in firms that do not offer insurance.

Risk and Insurance Purchasing

We first looked at the effect of risk on a worker's probability of obtaining any positive amount of private insurance coverage in different submarkets. We estimated so-called probit regressions, which determine the effect of risk on the probability of a worker's obtaining insurance.

Theory and Definitions. There are actually three different versions of the dependent variable that we consider to be of interest. We first estimate the effect of risk on the probability of being insured through one's own job. The second measure is the probability of obtaining insurance in connection with employment, either in one's own job or as a dependent of another person covered by employment-based group insurance. The final measure is the probability of having private insurance coverage from any source, either job-based or nongroup. The last measure is most important from a policy viewpoint, but the other two measures indicate whether there is behavior by insurers and employers in the group market that might have to be offset or adjusted. We do not look at the determinants of coverage for nonworkers.

We examine three subsets of the population, and we further divide each of them by income. Concentrating on full-time workers only, we look at everyone who is a worker in a large firm, everyone who is a worker in a small firm (with two to twenty-five employees), and everyone else (either self-employed or employed in a firm with only one employee). Again, we use total family income either above or below 300 percent of the poverty line to separate these subsets by income.

The explanatory variables in this regression include the demographic and locational variables used in the first stage of the premium regressions, along with a set of measures of employment income, occupation, and industry. (We hypothesize that this second set of variables will affect the likelihood of being insured but not the premium that would be quoted, given risk.)

Previous work on this subject is not extensive or conclusive. Using the 1984 Survey of Income and Program Participation, Buchmueller (1995) found some suggestion that male (but not female) workers reporting contemporaneous fair or poor health, difficulty with physical tasks, and work-related disabilities were less likely to be insured through their job than healthy workers. He concluded (presumably assuming that group premiums were pooled) that the absence of coverage was caused by employer screening in hiring decisions; an alternative interpretation, however, is that the absence of coverage led to poor health. Of course, the "job-lock" literature (Madrian 1994) argues for the opposite conclusion for workers already hired; high-risk workers are supposed to be less likely to leave jobs that carry health insurance than are low-risk workers.

Results—Probability of Being Insured. Table 4–1 shows sample means and regression results for the full set of explanatory variables for the pooled sample. Table 4–2 shows the coefficients on the risk measure for regressions for each of the "insurance market" subsamples and each of the three dependent variables, using the two alternative expense prediction specifications. We first show the effect on the probability of being insured of (log) predicted expenses, including the 1986 conditions. We then show results for the two different sets of prediction variables: the (log) predicted expenses using certain demographic and locational variables only, and the uncertain risk ratio of expenses predicted with the 1986-conditions variables and those using only the certain variables.

The data clearly indicate that there exist strong relationships between coverage and group size and between coverage and income. Coverage rates (from any source) for high-income workers are 83 percent, 90 percent, and 98 percent for nongroup, small-group, and large-group employees, respectively. For low-income workers, however, these coverage rates are 44 percent, 55 percent, and 87 percent, respectively. (The binary variables for group size and income in the full regression model shown in table 4–1 demonstrate this relationship explicitly.)

What about the relationship between risk and coverage? We first consider the high-income group. Given the size of the group, are high-risk, high-income persons less likely to obtain insurance coverage than low-risk persons with the same income? Perhaps surprisingly, the data presented in table 4–2 show no relationship between risk and the probability of obtaining coverage (in any of the three ways) for people at this income level. This result holds not only for group insurance but also for nongroup insurance. Although most people at these income levels are insured, about 11 percent in our sample are not. But

TABLE 4–1

MEAN STATISTICS AND REGRESSION COEFFICIENT ESTIMATES FOR PROBABILITY
OF INSURANCE COVERAGE FOR FULL-TIME (30 + HOURS) WORKERS, AGES
20–64

Variable	Mean Value	Probit Parameter Estimate
Employment-based policyholder	0.663	
Employment-based policyholder or dependent	0.793	
Any insurance/Intercept	0.857	− 2.274
Large firm (26 +)	0.630	1.229***
Small firm (2–25)	0.263	0.512***
Self-employed	0.107	
Family income above 300% of poverty line	0.619	0.738***
Predicted certain expenses: OLS model[a]	849.0	0.061
Uncertain (1986) risk ratio: OLS model	0.986	− 0.049
Male ages 20–24	0.061	0.057
Male ages 25–29	0.093	
Male ages 30–34	0.088	0.005
Male ages 35–39	0.085	0.007
Male ages 40–44	0.069	− 0.075
Male ages 45–49	0.045	− 0.094
Male ages 50–54	0.035	0.142
Male ages 55–59	0.035	0.033
Male ages 60–64	0.019	− 0.182
Female ages 20–24	0.058	0.235
Female ages 25–29	0.077	0.115
Female ages 30–34	0.079	0.278
Female ages 35–39	0.075	0.210
Female ages 40–44	0.060	0.316
Female ages 45–49	0.039	0.325
Female ages 50–54	0.036	0.415
Female ages 55–59	0.032	0.269
Female ages 60–64	0.017	0.551
Employment income[a]	20,183	0.020
Tenure	7.032	0.095***
Tenure squared	110.6	− 0.002***
Nonwhite	0.233	− 0.192***

(Table continues)

TABLE 4–1 (continued)

Variable	Mean Value	Probit Parameter Estimate
Education	12.88	0.089***
Married	0.659	0.490***
Professional/Management	0.299	0.208**
Labor union	0.143	0.362***
Agriculture, forestry, fishing	0.030	−0.301
Mining	0.009	−0.301
Construction	0.054	−0.500**
Manufacturing	0.229	0.133
Transportation, communication, utilities	0.064	0.056
Sales	0.163	−0.145
Finance, insurance, real estate	0.063	0.306
Repair services	0.053	−0.319
Personal services	0.033	−0.215
Entertainment, recreation	0.011	−0.132
Professional services	0.225	−0.027
Public administration	0.050	−0.118
Other industry	0.016	
New England—rural	0.005	0.305
New England—MSA	0.036	0.420
Mid-Atlantic—rural	0.022	−0.099
Mid-Atlantic—MSA	0.117	
East North Central—rural	0.039	0.065
East North Central—MSA	0.134	0.211*
West North Central—rural	0.038	0.291
West North Central—MSA	0.034	−0.092
South Atlantic—rural	0.083	−0.109
South Atlantic—MSA	0.136	−0.107
East South Central—rural	0.025	0.024
East South Central—MSA	0.042	−0.388**
West South Central—rural	0.027	−0.402**
West South Central—MSA	0.069	−0.369*
Mountain—rural	0.024	−0.213
Mountain—MSA	0.042	−0.220
Pacific—rural	0.013	−0.183
Pacific—MSA	0.114	−0.294**

TABLE 4–1 (continued)

Number of observations	5,145
Log likelihood	−1,358

***Significant at 0.01 or better.
**Significant at between 0.01 and 0.05.
*Significant at between 0.05 and 0.10.
a. In this probit regression and those that follow, both the log of predicted expenses and the log of worker income were used as independent variables.
NOTE: MSA = metropolitan statistical area.
SOURCE: 1987 NMES data.

neither the certain nor the uncertain determinants of risk are related to the likelihood of coverage. Indeed, the nonpoor higher risks do not even have to use dependent coverage or nongroup coverage in order to have the same likelihood of obtaining insurance as nonpoor lower risks. For these households, neither higher premiums for high risks nor anything else appears to affect the *relative* likelihood of being covered.

What might account for this uniformity in the probability of being covered across *all* insurance categories, including the supposedly risk-rated nongroup market? There are two interpretations of the results, one benign and the other less so. The benign interpretation is that high-income people are able to obtain insurance at prices they are usually willing to pay, at all risk levels, in all markets. For example, even if the nongroup premium should increase with risk, high-risk consumers recognize the greater value of insurance to them and so are willing to pay more for it. Perhaps also, through the mechanisms described earlier, they are exposed only to moderate variations in premiums with risk (even in nongroup markets), and these variations are not large enough to selectively deter the purchase of coverage.

The less benign interpretation is that high premiums do confront some high risks who have not been able to disguise their risk level, and those persons do respond by dropping coverage. But other high risks engage in adverse selection. They do secure coverage at premiums that are low relative to their risks, and this shortfall causes premiums to rise across the board. The resulting elevation of premiums over expected benefits for low risks causes an equal number of low-risk persons to drop coverage. It is the average risks who are most likely to be insured, but the implication is that there is no monotonic increase in the probability of becoming insured that is related to risk.

TABLE 4-2
PROBABILITY OF INSURANCE COVERAGE FOR
VARIOUS SUBSAMPLES: EXPECTED-EXPENSE COEFFICIENTS FROM PROBIT REGRESSIONS

A: Large-Group/High-Income, N = 2,164

	Linear OLS Model			Two-Part Square-Root Model		
	Log predicted expenses, before 1987	Log predicted expenses, certain variables	Uncertain risk ratio, before 1987	Log predicted expenses, before 1987	Log predicted expenses, certain variables	Uncertain risk ratio, before 1987
Employment-based policyholder	0.00	0.24	0.04	0.20	−0.46	0.19
Employment-based insurance	0.02	0.19	0.00	0.09	2.29	0.05
Any insurance	−0.03	2.39	−0.07	−0.01	1.09	0.02

B: Small-Group/High-Income, N = 709

	Linear OLS Model			Two-Part Square-Root Model		
	Log predicted expenses, before 1987	Log predicted expenses, certain variables	Uncertain risk ratio, before 1987	Log predicted expenses, before 1987	Log predicted expenses, certain variables	Uncertain risk ratio, before 1987
Employment-based policyholder	0.09	1.37**	0.01	−0.02	2.02	−0.03
Employment-based insurance	−0.19	−0.20	−0.07	−0.06	−2.67	−0.03
Any insurance	0.04	−0.64	0.20	0.48	−2.20	0.27

C: Self-Employed/High-Income, N = 311

	Linear OLS Model			Two-Part Square-Root Model		
	Log predicted expenses, before 1987	Log predicted expenses, certain variables	Uncertain risk ratio, before 1987	Log predicted expenses, before 1987	Log predicted expenses, certain variables	Uncertain risk ratio, before 1987
Employment-based policyholder	n.a.	n.a.	n.a.	n.a.	n.a.	n.a.
Employment-based insurance	0.19	0.80	0.21	0.61	−17.45**	0.48
Any insurance	−0.22	1.47	−0.27	−0.06	−8.99	0.08

(Table continues)

TABLE 4–2 (continued)

D: Large-Group/Low-Income, N = 1,079

	Linear OLS Model			Two-Part Square-Root Model		
	Log predicted expenses, before 1987	Log predicted expenses, certain variables	Uncertain risk ratio, before 1987	Log predicted expenses, before 1987	Log predicted expenses, certain variables	Uncertain risk ratio, before 1987
Employment-based policyholder	−0.10	0.18	0.01	0.11	0.71	0.14
Employment-based insurance	−0.13	−0.22	−0.01	0.02	2.52	0.06
Any insurance	−0.14	−0.61	−0.01	0.13	1.49	0.15

E: Small-Group/Low-Income, N = 645

	Linear OLS Model			Two-Part Square-Root Model		
	Log predicted expenses, before 1987	Log predicted expenses, certain variables	Uncertain risk ratio, before 1987	Log predicted expenses, before 1987	Log predicted expenses, certain variables	Uncertain risk ratio, before 1987
Employment-based policyholder	−0.21**	−0.12	−0.24**	−0.58**	−5.09*	−0.41**
Employment-based insurance	−0.13	−0.26	−0.19**	−0.49*	−5.43**	−0.39**
Any insurance	−0.10	−0.11	−0.13	−0.49*	−5.63**	−0.30*

F: Self-Employed/Low-Income, N = 237

	Linear OLS Model			Two-Part Square-Root Model		
	Log predicted expenses, before 1987	Log predicted expenses, certain variables	Uncertain risk ratio, before 1987	Log predicted expenses, before 1987	Log predicted expenses, certain variables	Uncertain risk ratio, before 1987
Employment-based policyholder	n.a.	n.a.	n.a.	n.a.	n.a.	n.a.
Employment-based insurance	−0.36	1.92	−0.02	−0.58	−18.48	−0.22
Any insurance	−0.19	−0.96	−0.15	−0.39	−16.44**	−0.06

**Significant at between 0.01 and 0.05.
*Significant at between 0.05 and 0.10.
SOURCE: 1987 NMES data.

Under both scenarios, of course, some nonpoor people remain uninsured, perhaps because of lack of demand, or perhaps because they face premiums that are high regardless of the risk level. Even here, however, variation in risk per se is not the problem, and the proportion of moderate- to high-income people who chose not to be insured was, in the period represented, quite small.

The results for low-income workers are quite different. High-risk, low-income workers in small groups were found to be both less likely to be insured by their employer and less likely to be insured from any source, relative to low risks. The results, shown in table 4–2, panel E, indicate a statistically significant and negative aspect of risk level on the probability of obtaining insurance in various ways. Some of this effect is attributable to the certain determinants of risk, and some of it to the presence of chronic conditions.

We do not know the specific reason for this result. It may be that low-income high risks are less able to disguise or overcome that fact in seeking employment; they may be less able to locate another job with coverage, or to argue for themselves. Alternatively, and plausibly, given the (absolutely) high premiums, people at this level of income or wealth may consider charity or bad-debt care as a preferable way to obtain care.

Of course, these low-income persons are also less likely to be insured at any risk level than were high-income people. Relative to the total effect of income per se, the *differential* effect on high risks is rather moderate—and, of course, it is offset by a relatively greater likelihood of being insured among low-income low risks. Even the latter group, however, has a probability of being uninsured that many would find unacceptably high. This higher probability is perhaps attributable to a number of influences: low-income workers are more likely to work in small firms where coverage is expensive and are more likely to decline coverage that is costly relative to charity care.

Wage Incidence and Risk in Group Insurance

The final important empirical issue concerns the distribution of the cost of group insurance over the workers in a group. External (non-self-insured) group insurers usually charge a total premium to the group, not to specific individuals in it.

Theory and Definitions. Insurers or analysts may divide that premium by the number of covered lives for calculation purposes, but there is no necessary implication about how insurers bill employers, or about how each employee's command over other goods and services should be reduced. But both economic analysis and common sense do suggest that much of the cost of insurance will come out of employee wages. When the group is self-insured, there is even less reason to assume that the employer spreads this cost perfectly evenly over each employee's wages.

This point raises the most complex and least well understood conceptual and empirical issue in the analysis of group insurance: how employers and the labor market adjust wages when employers pay part of workers' compensation in the form of group insurance. Here we explore several plausible models to show that the answer to this question can be quite different depending on which analytic model actually holds.

We are going to assume (as seems realistic) that we do observe some groups, large and small, that provide insurance to all their workers, and that they contain some above-average and some below-average insured risks. One model might be called the "laser-beam" model. In this approach, in the spirit of studies by Gruber (1994) and Sheiner (1994), the employer searches out and pinpoints the high-risk employee and reduces that employee's "disposable income" (through a higher employee premium or a lower money wage) by the amount of the extra expected benefit. If this happens, it is easy to see that the cost the employee bears does *not* depend on the amount of pooling or averaging available to the group; a high-risk person in a very large group will be "charged" as much as a high-risk person in a smaller group. That is because the relevant magnitude is the *marginal* premium for this person's coverage, not the average premium per employee paid by the group. The higher charge will generally be reflected in a lower wage, not a higher employee-paid premium.

Indeed, if larger groups are self-insured while smaller groups are less accurately risk-rated, the premium actually paid (in some sense) by the high-risk person under the laser-beam model could actually be larger in large groups than in small ones. The fact that converting one employee from average to high risk raises the average premium by much less in a large group than in a small one is irrelevant if the high-risk employee can be singled out for lower wages or for a higher employee premium. To fail to do so when it is possible will cut into the employer's profits.

Another model might be called a "competitive labor-market"

model. Assume that all workers are equally productive, that the loading is the same for all groups, and that workers can take jobs at any firm. Also assume that, because of administrative costs or for equity reasons, workers of different risks must receive the same money wage within any firm. It then follows that "disposable income" (wages minus employee premiums) in equilibrium must be the same in all firms that continue to operate. Consider a very large group with approximately the average experience as a benchmark. The "law of one price" holds that in a competitive labor market, all other employers who remain in business will offer in equilibrium the same net compensation as the benchmark firm: labor must be paid the same amount in all competitive job opportunities. A small group with the good luck to have no high-risk workers will not pay higher wages or charge lower employee premiums than the benchmark, since there is no need to do so to attract workers. An unlucky small group, with more than the average number of high-risk members, that wants to remain in business will not pay lower wages or charge higher employee premiums, since it then could not retain its workers (of whatever level of risk). In equilibrium, it will be small-group *employers*—not the workers—who pay what Bandian and Lewin (1995) call "the real [additional] premium for someone with chronic illness."

Readers may be willing to accept the competitive labor-market prediction for the lucky small group, but we suspect that they will question the prediction for the unlucky small group. Won't employers who are forced to absorb high premiums go out of business? Some will, but other small employers who have some other competitive advantage that offsets high insurance costs will survive. Won't employers fire these high-risk workers and hire lower-risk ones? Perhaps, but if we are to observe these high-risk insured workers anywhere, someone must be hiring them. The point is that the surviving employers with high-risk insured work forces must be using up some of their differential advantage, or "rent." Perhaps they hired the high-risk workers before they became high risks, trained them, and now would have to bear the cost of retraining if they were to replace them. Or there may be specialized skills or locational advantages to these workers.

It is clear that paying lower wages or charging higher premiums to all members of the high-risk group, including those who are not high risk, cannot be an equilibrium, since then the non-high-risk workers will depart. This pushes groups toward homogeneity in terms of risk, but as long as the benchmark group is willing to hire high-risk workers, no group of above-average risks paying lower than average wages can be stable.

These last observations suggest that some more complex models are possible: for example, that large groups pay good wages and charge average premiums to the high risks they have already hired, but refuse to hire new applicants who are high risks. But such "sorting" models are both complex and difficult to construct in an assuredly realistic fashion, given our current state of knowledge. The main conclusion of this argument, however, still holds true: in a world where groups are charged premiums that vary to a greater or lesser extent with risk, it is by no means certain that small groups that survive will differ from large groups. Either both types of groups will be "risk rating" their employees equally (the laser-beam model), or neither group will be doing so (the competitive-labor-market model). The fundamental logical problem is that a world where employers compete for the same workers but treat some differently from others cannot exist. If such a world does exist, it must be unstable.

Results. Since theory cannot settle the matter, we turn to data to resolve it. In the analysis of the NMES data, however, we do not have the benefit of an exogenous source of variation in insurance coverage, with workers or firms randomly assigned to coverage or no coverage. The most straightforward test would be to see whether money wages are lower for insured high-risk workers than for insured low-risk workers. But it is quite possible that some of the risk characteristics that would affect expected expenses might also affect productivity; a worker with a chronic condition may miss work more frequently and earn lower wages, other things being equal. To provide a benchmark of "pure-productivity-based wages," we therefore examine the relationship (if any) between risk and wages for people who are not obtaining employment-based insurance through their own jobs. Such persons may be uninsured, or they might be covered as dependents on someone else's policy. That is, we compare the effect of risk on wage earnings among the job-insured and among the job-uninsured, and we look for any difference in the effect. Such a difference-in-difference approach should test whether risk related to insurance cost would affect wages.

We therefore specify a traditional wage regression, controlling for occupation, industry, and location. Some variables serve as potential productivity-wage bargain adjusters, as well as affecting insurance costs. One such variable is experience. The NMES survey asks each worker the number of years worked with the current firm ("tenure"). (It does not provide data on the total experience of a worker with all past employers.) Although wages usually rise with seniority or experience, so do age and expected expenses. Hence, a finding that wages rose more rapidly with tenure in uninsured firms than in insured firms would imply that the incidence of premiums varied with age. The key insight is this: some of the positive effects of an additional year of tenure on productivity and wages would be eaten up by higher expected medical expenses.

A similar comment applies to gender. If women are discriminated against, or are simply less productive, wages may be lower for women than for men (given occupation and tenure). Since women generally have somewhat higher medical expenses at a given age than men, one hypothesizes that the partial effect of female gender on wages should be higher among insured workers. But the difference in expected expense related to gender is ordinarily much smaller (over the range of observations) than that related to age. A thirty-five-year-old woman may have medical expenses 25 percent higher than a man's, but a sixty-year-old worker will have average expenses two to four times greater than a twenty-five-year-old's.

Empirically, we include both tenure and tenure squared in our (log of) wage regression, and control for age and gender using three different model specifications. The first demographic specification simply uses the five-year age intervals interacted with gender, as with the prior analysis. The aggregate data suggest that age affects wages in a "lumpy" fashion; wages do rise with age for men, though not uniformly or proportionately. For women, wages are at first flat, and then they fall slightly with age before turning upward. Our second demographic specification uses five more aggregated cells: young men (under age thirty), old men (over fifty), old women (over fifty), other men, and other women. The final demographic specification uses only a binary variable, and only for females.

Finally, to test for any effect of "uncertain" risk on wages attributable to the onset of chronic conditions, we again use one of the following two approaches: either the (log of) predicted expenses, including the prior-period variables, or both the (log of) predicted certain expenses and the uncertain risk ratio.

The results indicate three things. First, there is no evidence that the effect on wages of uncertain risk, however measured, is significant

TABLE 4–3
EFFECT OF YEARS OF JOB EXPERIENCE (TENURE) ON WAGES FOR EMPLOYEES
WITH AND WITHOUT INSURANCE FROM THEIR OWN JOBS

	All Firms		Small Firms	
	Own Insurance	Not Own Insurance	Own Insurance	Not Own Insurance
Demographic Specification: Five-Year Intervals Interacted with Gender				
Estimated effect[a]	0.019**	0.028**	0.012**	0.027**
Adjusted *R*-square	0.354	0.314	0.213	0.289
Demographic Specification: Five Aggregate Age-Gender Cells				
Estimated effect	0.022*	0.028*	0.017	0.027
Adjusted *R*-square	0.348	0.313	0.207	0.291
Demographic Specification: Gender Binary Only				
Estimated effect	0.024*	0.029*	0.020*	0.030*
Adjusted *R*-square	0.340	0.305	0.205	0.276
Number of observations	3,398	1,199	627	727

NOTE: Estimates are evaluated at the mean value of job tenure (6.78 years) for the pooled samples. The model specification for log (wages) includes both tenure and tenure squared terms, so that the reported Estimated Effect equals $b_1 + 2b_2 \times T_{mean}$, where b_1 and b_2 are the tenure and tenure-squared coefficients, respectively.
a. Significance in the first-order difference between the Own Insurance and Not Own Insurance groups:
**Significant at between 0.01 and 0.05.
 *Significant at between 0.05 and 0.10.
SOURCE: 1987 NMES data.

at all or is different for those who do or do not obtain group insurance through their jobs. Second, female gender has the same negative effect on wages for job-insured and job-uninsured workers; employers do not cut women's wages (relative to men's) by more when they are insured than when they are not. Third, however, and perhaps most significant, the effect of job tenure on wage income *is* much smaller for insured workers than for uninsured ones; these results are shown in table 4–3 for each of the three demographic specifications. For instance, based on the five age-gender-cell specifications, wages for a typical employee rise annually by 2.8 percent in a firm from which insurance is not obtained, while that same individual's wages would increase by only 2.2 percent annually in a firm providing insurance. Additionally, the results suggest that this tenure effect is stronger for small groups than for large ones.

These results are consistent with previous work. It appears that for some risk characteristics, there is variation related to risk in the money wage paid to employee-insured workers. As noted above, Gruber (1994) found that when all employers in a state were required to provide coverage for maternity benefits, the wages of women of childbearing age and their husbands fell. Sheiner (1994) found that wages declined as insured workers grew older, other things being equal. Apparently, then, some worker characteristics that all employers can easily observe and build into the wage structure do result in risk adjustment of wages by as much as (or even more than) the difference in expected expense. These risks are *not* pooled in employment-based insurance—especially not in small firms.

In contrast, characteristics that are more difficult to observe, such as the presence of a chronic condition that does not affect the worker's ability to work, do not appear to lead to wage offsets. Perhaps there are administrative costs and labor-relations costs associated with trying to penalize a high-risk worker. Or perhaps workers prefer firms that pool these uncertain risks.

5

❖

The Effect of the Tax Subsidy
on Risk Pooling

Does the tax subsidy to employment-based health insurance cause the amount of risk rating (the extent to which a household's net payments vary with expected expenses) to be lower than would be the case in the absence of the tax subsidy? Or does it bribe consumers into letting their employer select and control their insurance, often unnecessarily frustrating individuals' desires? Different commentators have given affirmative answers to both questions. In this chapter we reconsider these questions in the light of the empirical work just described.

As already discussed, the conventional wisdom concerning pooling is that employee premiums for employment-based insurance do not vary with risk within the firm, while premiums are alleged to be strongly risk-related in the individual-insurance market. In effect, commentators concerned about pooling compare an optimistic view of today's group insurance market with a pessimistic view of today's individual insurance market. They observe that pooling appears to be greater in the former than in the latter, and they come to the worrisome conclusion that in the absence of the tax subsidy to employment-based group insurance, a sizable portion (if not all) of the group market would become like the individual market, and pooling would suffer.

In this chapter, we show that both types of views must be modified. These simple arguments are not conclusive for at least three reasons. The first two deal with empirical facts already presented in this study; the third deals with ambiguity about the hypothesized behavior.

1. When wage adjustments are taken into account, the employment-based group market does not itself pool some important variations in risk, either within firms or across firms.
2. Premiums in the individual market are far from perfectly risk related, and the degree of risk rating is a choice variable; there is a substantial amount of pooling.
3. People may not drop out of employment-based groups if the differential subsidy were to fall. The preferred alternative to partially pooled group insurance with a differential tax subsidy may not be individual insurance, but may rather still be partially pooled group insurance without a differential tax subsidy, because of the strong administrative-cost advantages to group insurance.

We begin with pooling. Some commentators criticize employer choice and argue instead for "individually owned" insurance. They assume that employees will not get what they want in group insurance and that it might be only a little more costly to allow them to choose their insurance individually. Yet we know that group insurance is much less costly (in terms of administrative costs) than today's individual insurance. So even without a subsidy, group insurance might be preferred.

But does the tax subsidy require (or depend on) pooling of insurance costs across workers in a firm? The answer to that question depends on what firms had to do to qualify for the tax subsidy. The tax laws themselves were, in the late 1980s period we studied, actually not very restrictive. The employer had to set up a process by which premiums were paid, although this payment could flow first into a cafeteria plan and then to insurers.[5] Group plans, in principle, had to be uniform for broad classes of employees; they could not favor certain "key man" employees.

After the passage of the Americans with Disabilities Act in 1990, the employer could not discriminate against disabled employees in hiring or in payment of wages. But even here, actuarially justifiable coverage or premium adjustments could be made (Sabota 1999). Risk factors *not* related to a worker's job-related disability (for example, disabilities of family members or nondisabling chronic conditions of workers) could legally be accounted for in employee premiums (although they rarely were), as long as they were actuarially based. Laws prohibiting hiring or wage discrimination on the basis of age or gender had to be observed.

The main point is that the tax law and other laws prior to the Health Insurance Portability and Accountability Act (HIPAA) of 1996 placed relatively few limits on the way in which an employer could vary wages or the premium charged for insurance. It would have been legal to charge higher premiums to older workers or those with chronic conditions, as long as those characteristics were not proxies for highly paid status, and as long as the premium variations were justifiable. The federal and state laws (contrary to the Gruber-Madrian [1997] assertion) did not then prohibit wage or benefit discrimination across workers in general; they only required that discrimination in premiums be actuarially based and not a device for rewarding higher-income employees. Employee premiums could be (largely) tax-shielded by setting up a cafeteria benefits plan. It would even be possible to put tax-shielded funds into the cafeteria plan and then allow employees to purchase risk-rated nongroup insurance with the funds in that account: even age or gender could be used as criteria, as long as they were actuarially based.

The reach of other discrimination laws was limited to a small set of protected risk categories. Even these categories could still be associated with legal de facto discrimination if they were correlated with different job categories; for instance, firms were permitted to pay more to workers with seniority, even though this practice might discriminate against young workers or women. State laws might extend further, but the Employee Retirement Income Security Act (ERISA)–protected groups need not comply with these laws.

While there are some additional limits on risk rating employee premiums or wages under the tax law current in 1999, even those limits are relatively mild. The rules in HIPAA, passed in 1997, further limit risk discrimination in group insurance based on health status, while having little or no effect on the nongroup market. Paradoxically, the law prohibited explicit risk rating in situations in which it was known to be rare, while continuing to permit it in the situation where it was thought to be the worst problem.

The surprising revelation is that, despite the fact that the tax advantages offered to group insurance neither required risk pooling nor forbade risk rating, we did not observe any appreciable number of groups engaging in risk rating (Harrington and Niehaus 1999). The argument in what follows is this: since groups did not risk-rate under a tax-subsidy scheme that permitted risk rating, they should not logically seek to initiate more risk rating if the subsidies were to be removed.

Toward a Model

The employment-based group performs two separate tasks. First, it chooses which insurance plan or plans will be made available to its members. Second, it decides how the cost of that insurance will be distributed over members of the group. It is the performance of the second task that is related to risk pooling, but it is the first task that provides the rationale for the formation of insurance groups.

To begin, consider a population of workers who all have the same risk level (expected medical expenses, given insurance coverage), but who have different preferences for health insurance. These preferences may vary either because there is variation in risk aversion or because there is variation in the disutility attached to nonmonetary devices used to control moral hazard. Group-insurance purchasing, we will assume, will always cause any insurance plan (or set of insurance plans smaller than the full set available in the market) to be offered at administrative loadings below those of individual insurance; group insurance is assumed always to be less costly. Administrative cost savings over nongroup insurance are greater the larger the group and the smaller the number of insurance options offered, but they are assumed to be positive even for the smallest group.

For the moment, assume as well that the set of persons potentially included in an employment group is predetermined. What then predicts whether group insurance will be offered and the number and variety of plans? One possible decision rule is that the group should do what is efficient. This means that it should solve what is essentially a local public-goods problem (Goldstein and Pauly 1976). It determines the optimal plan to be offered if only the one is offered, if only two are offered, and so forth. The more plans that are offered, the higher the administrative cost, but the closer on average each person's plan will be to that person's most preferred plan. Plans are priced efficiently with a fixed-dollar employer contribution equal to the premium of the lowest-priced plan offered. Then the optimal mix of plans is that variety that minimizes the sum of administrative costs and the implicit cost associated with deviations from each person's preferred alternative.

Once the optimal group plan (or set of plans) is determined in this model, it will be offered if it yields higher aggregate utility than the set of workers could obtain in the individual market. Again, the trade-off between preference satisfaction and administrative cost will come into play. Group insurance will be less likely to be optimal if the group is small (so that the administrative cost savings, positive by definition, are relatively small) and preferences heterogeneous (so that deviations from one's preferred plan under group insurance is large). Group size interacts with heterogeneity, since the smaller the group, the more costly it is to offer multiple plans.

In this model, group insurance will often be offered even in the absence of a tax subsidy, because workers as a group are better off under group insurance than under individual insurance purchasing. But if a tax subsidy is offered to employment-based group insurance and not to individually chosen insurance, it will have two main effects. First, for those work forces that would have chosen group insurance anyway, the levels of coverage will be more generous or the strictness of managed care restrictions will be weaker. Second, some work forces that chose not to offer group insurance will now do so, since the tax subsidy will both offset higher administrative costs in the group (but not in the individual market) and will, more important, offset the less accurate matching of options and preferences in group insurance. A secondary effect, since the tax subsidy underwrites administrative costs, is that the group will be induced to offer more options.

All these conclusions follow because we assumed that the original employer or group decision was to offer the efficient level and mixture of insurance. This may not necessarily happen: if the group is run by a union, it may well choose to emphasize the kinds of policies preferred by whatever subgroup dominates the union (usually middle-aged males). If it is run by the employer, the employer may focus on offering low-cost plans or, even with a correct view of incidence, may favor plans preferred by those workers who are more responsive to the total compensation package. It is more difficult to predict what a differential tax subsidy would do in the presence of inefficient choice, but presumably it would still encourage more group plans, even if they were inefficient.

But if employers or unions do make the optimal choice for the group, this way of looking at the problem carries a strong implication:

it may be efficient to require all employees to "belong" to the group (in the sense of having part of their compensation directed to the premium of the group-chosen plan); it may well be inefficient to give employees the guaranteed option of taking the equivalent amount of cash instead and using it to buy insurance more to their liking or to buy something other than insurance. The reason is that employees who drop out raise the administrative costs paid by those who remain. In this sense, what is individually rational may be collectively irrational: the gain to the employee who drops out may fall well short of the costs imposed on those who remain.

To construct the other half of the model, we reverse the assumptions and assume that all persons have the same utility functions but differ by risk level. Even in this case they may still prefer different levels of insurance coverage, but let us assume that the variation in preferences based on risk is sufficiently small that groups will optimally choose to offer just one insurance policy. What would happen if the tax subsidy were dropped? The desired level of coverage would surely fall, but then what?

There are two stories of how group insurance might be affected. One version imagines that after this change, employers or unions would choose to stop providing such coverage. The other version concentrates on individual worker decisions to move from firms offering group insurance to firms that do not offer it. In the latter case, we will assume that the utility function is such that everyone would turn to the individual-insurance market for coverage as a last resort.

To consider the first version: if an employer chose to offer group coverage with a tax subsidy, why would the employer decide to drop that coverage just because employees were taxed on the employer contribution? To provide any answer at all to this question, we have to make some assumptions about the incidence of employer-premium payments. If we assume that (a) these payments come out of what would otherwise be employer profits; but that (b) employers choose to "give" coverage, either because of concern for employees' welfare or because they think it increases employee productivity; then (c) there should be no change. Employers pay no more taxes than before; why should they care about an increase in employee taxes?

Economists would generally assume, in contrast, that the cost of insurance nominally paid by the employer is actually borne by the employee in lower wages (Pauly 1997). Since these lower money wages originally led to lower taxes but now do not, the gain to the employees from group insurance would fall by the amount of the lost tax subsidy. It is the employees—some of them, at least—who might want a change. By assumption, however, the cost of obtaining insurance through a group, even without a tax subsidy, is lower than the cost of getting it individually. Financially speaking, after the tax break is removed, group insurance is not as advantageous as it was. It still remains a better deal for all employees combined, however, than would canceling the insurance, being paid in cash, and then buying the more expensive individual insurance.

But even if, on average, employees would lose, might some low risks not gain from dropping out of the group, going to employers who pay all compensation in cash, and then buying insurance in the risk-rated individual market? This is the argument made by Bandian and Lewin (1995). What it requires is that for some employees, the cost of individual insurance is less than the increase in wages from moving to an employer who offers no coverage. Would this ever happen?

Here is a case in which it *could*. Suppose that all employee wages were reduced by equal dollar amounts in the group-insurance regime, and suppose that the employers offering no insurance are willing to pay the same amount as total compensation for each employee. The low-risk employees will switch if the additional loading they would pay under individual insurance is less than the difference between their expected actuarially fair insurance premium and the per-employee premium payment under group insurance.

Would this ever actually happen? The cost of individual insurance is about twice as great as the cost of the same coverage in a medium or large group. Benefit costs per worker increase by a factor of three or four to one from the youngest age to the oldest age (under sixty-five) workers, with the ramp-up most strongly occurring after age forty-five or so. Based on NMES data, however, the only group that would have expected benefit costs to be half of the average (and just barely so) would be males up to age forty-five with absolutely no chronic conditions. Moreover, at present, companies that do not offer insurance often pay lower total compensation than companies that do. We conclude that only among smaller firms might there be some advantage from low risks dropping out, and that advantage would apply only to a relatively small segment of the work force.

Even this conclusion needs to be tempered. As discussed earlier, accumulating evidence suggests that the effect of age on health benefit costs is already offset in the form of lower wages for older insured workers and higher wages for younger insured workers. Thus, the net gain in money wages for younger workers who move from a firm offering coverage to a firm that does not might be well below the average cost of insurance per worker, even if total compensation costs were the same. Younger workers would see wages in firms not offering insurance increased only by *their* expected expenses, not by the average level of such expenses. If "rewards" were adjusted for age and gender, the difference between expected expenses for a person with no chronic conditions and for the average person is definitely less than the additional loading attached to individual insurance. Thus, if the only difference is financial, the reward from dropping out is likely to be small.

As noted above, however, there is another reward: in the individual market you get the policy you want. This closer matching could potentially drive low-risk employees out of a group. If, for example, younger workers really wanted catastrophic coverage that the group refused to offer, removing the tax subsidy might make the difference. Still, such defections seem unlikely to drive up premiums (drive down wages) of the remaining group members to an appreciable extent.

The only empirical evidence about the effect of tax subsidies on the probability of obtaining any coverage comes from the work of Gruber and Poterba (1994), which analyzed the effect of changes in permitted tax deductibility for health insurance by the self-employed. They found that coverage did indeed decline when tax deductibility fell. In the case of the self-employed, however, there is usually no issue of pooling in group insurance; they usually buy in the nongroup market. In effect, when their tax subsidy was cut, some opted not for risk-rated coverage but for no coverage at all. In the case of the subsidy to group coverage, surely it is also responsible for inducing some people to stay insured. If the subsidy disappeared, they would drop coverage as well. Paying a subsidy to coverage, regardless of how obtained, may be much more important than preserving the near-exclusive subsidy to group coverage.

Who Wins?

There is another, even stronger, logical argument. Assume that the number of high-risk people with chronic conditions in a group is never large enough to motivate lower risks in the group to screen for the high risks. This is a plausible assumption because until recently, nothing prevented groups from doing risk rating, even with a subsidy of screening costs. This screening cost represents the cost of proving or determining that a low risk really is a low risk. If the low risk turns to the nongroup market, the same screening cost would have to be incurred there and, in addition, the administrative costs would be higher for other reasons. So a low risk could never do better outside of a group than within a group, even if the group is not risk rating. That is, *if* low risks could gain by dropping out, they could gain even more by having the group risk-rate. Since groups do not risk-rate, however, it must be true that low risks would not gain by dropping out.

Does the tax subsidy change this? Not directly; group insurance will always remain superior. Of course, jobs are not in reality differentiated solely by the provision of health insurance. Removing the tax subsidy will raise the tax on some jobs, and in some cases employees may now find a job without insurance to be more attractive.

What about the alternative view, that insurance ought to be individually chosen and individually owned, regardless of what employers or employees prefer? The answer is implicit in what has already been said: because group insurance can lower the price of insurance in real terms, not just provide the setting for a tax break, *often* it may be better for employees to let the employer arrange things. While the great majority of employees might therefore be expected to select insurance obtained through the group voluntarily by agreeing to "spend" their own money, this arrangement can be fragile. If, by mistake or caprice, some employees decided not to use the group, that would raise the cost of group insurance to the remainder, driving some away. A real death spiral might ensue; the fragility of equilibrium to variations in individual behavior is great when economics of scale are present, as they are here. There is a stable alternative: let the participation in group insurance (with no backing-out allowed) be part of the contract offered to, and freely entered into by, employees. That is, "individual ownership" ought ideally to be an option, not a government-enforced obligation. Labor contracting should be left up to employers and employees, with no tax distortions or legal intrusions.

Another way to look at voluntarily contracted, compulsory group insurance is as a device for dealing with temporary variations in risk. Insurance cannot work well if people can cancel or cut back insurance when they are well and enter the market and expand coverage when they get sick. Compulsory group insurance inhibits such opportunistic behavior; even though insurance policies typically apply for only one year, group membership can convert this into a much longer-term contract.

We must have an idea of when a group will community rate (or in some way deviate from individual-employee risk rating or private-individual insurance) and when it will not. We assume that group insurance is always administratively less costly than private individual insurance, and that employees have some desire for protection against risk rating on a short-term basis. We also assume that, at either the group or the individual loading, everyone will prefer to be insured rather than uninsured. If high-risk conditions are temporary, then an equilibrium in which premiums are constant is feasible. No employee who is low-risk will be attracted by another employer who offers no insurance but higher wages, because the risk of becoming a high risk will be greater at such an employer, and therefore undesirable to every worker. Different buyers may choose different degrees of smoothing, but this will just lead to sorting across firms. Likewise, if all firms offering insurance pay lower wages to employees as they age, there will be no reason for younger workers to drop out or fail to choose a group, because the alternative of higher wages and no insurance is less desirable to them (since individual insurance for low risks is more expensive than what they are paying in the group).

Thus, for there to be a problem with risk rating, high-risk conditions must be permanent. Even if all young workers start out at the same risk level, over time those who do not contract chronic conditions will come to realize that the value to them of continuation in the group is diminishing, especially because Medicare will eventually protect them against the higher cost of chronic conditions.

If employees will not drop out, would employers ever see increased gain from dropping coverage after the tax subsidy is removed? Those employers whose costs and risks are close to the average will not gain, based on the argument presented earlier: there is no additional demand for uninsured jobs. But what about employers whose groups contain above-average proportions of high risks, generating a cost that the employer (capital owner) must absorb if the worker is to continue to be employed? Will dropping coverage increase their profits after the tax subsidy is removed (when doing so would not have increased profits when the subsidy was present)? The answer is possibly yes. Removing the tax subsidy reduces the difference in value between an uninsured job and an insured job. The employer might then be better off dropping insurance and raising wages; with no subsidy, some high-risk workers might not mind. Given some number of high-risk employees, this advantage is more likely to be positive the smaller the group, but is likely to be rare.

Efficiency of Employment-based Groups and the Tax Subsidy

There are two main reasons why employment-based groups may be inefficient. They may be too small, or they may be too heterogeneous. Obviously, if the group is limited to the firm or the establishment, a sufficiently small size will increase administrative costs. There might in theory be some larger group to which workers belong, such as a professional or recreational association, whose true cost of providing them with health insurance is actually much less than at the small firm. But because only payments in the employment-based setting are eligible for the favorable tax treatment, the inefficient outcome occurs.

Heterogeneity will lead to fewer persons getting exactly the insurance they want. It can in theory even lead to a decision to provide no group insurance at all if some people are worse off with insurance than without it. For example, suppose a group is split between low-wage workers who dislike inpatient care and higher-wage workers who prefer inpatient care, and suppose the group is small enough that it will optimally have only one insurance policy. The best policy might be one in which only one group will choose to participate—but then the low take-up ratio will mean that the insurer is unwilling to write group coverage.

Whether there is no insurance offered or just a less-than-ideal mix, efficiency could be improved if people would group in different ways: lower-income hospital haters in one group, and higher-income hospital lovers in another. Again, however, even if such groups are feasible and efficient, they might be rejected, because they lack tax breaks.

Since the employment-based group could have risk-rated but did not, we conclude that risk pooling will remain unchanged in those employment-based groups that remain. But what will the alternative sources of insurance, used by erstwhile employees of small firms, be like, and how much pooling or risk rating will they do?

We have little to go on here that is directly relevant, although we can see some suggestions in the behavior of other insurance markets. There are a few possible bases for alternative grouping arrangements. One approach is to create a larger employment-based group, which we hope can offer more choices at lower premiums. We have several kinds of experience with this type of arrangement. One is the craft-union model, in which a trade union (a larger compulsory aggregate) arranges coverage for the carpenters, plumbers, or electricians who work for many small firms. Except for issues of governance, such health and welfare funds seem to work reasonably well. Replicating the compulsory membership outside the trade-union setting is a problem, though. The other experience is that while some employees have associations easily available, others do not. There is an American Economic Association, but so far as we know no American Administrative Assistants Association.

A second approach is to group businesses together in a purpose-created buying or administrative group. The Health Mart concept seems close to this, as do groups like the Council of Small Enterprises in Cleveland.

A third approach is for people to buy insurance as individuals, perhaps with a small amount of initial filtering. For instance, the auto insurers GEICO and State Farm originally marketed to government employees and farmers, respectively, while the American Association of Retired Persons (AARP) requires attainment of a certain age and purchase of its magazine.

This last arrangement deserves some additional comment. In other insurance, so-called direct selling has reduced administrative costs compared with the more costly independent or American Agent method, getting loadings down into the 25-percent-of-premium range—less than the value for the typical individual health insurance (Pauly, Kunreuther, and Kleindorfer 1986). In addition, the requirement that the insured be a full-time worker may serve as an effective screening device, in terms of both risk and reliability in premium payment.

This difference alone could lead to behavior in such prescreened or "semi-group" firms' being very different from today's nongroup insurance market—or, at least, from the common perception of it. Since it is costly to identify high risks (so as to charge them more or refuse them coverage), lower risks will be willing to bear the cost of doing so, other things being equal, only if high risks are present in a sufficiently high proportion. The current nongroup market accepts applications from anyone, and its high premiums (relative to benefits) alone ensure that the applicants are likely to be high-risk if they are not highly risk-averse. In contrast, a semi-group seller would have sorted out many of the high risks with an innocent requirement that buyers be full-time workers. Moreover, if removal of the tax subsidy causes the collapse of small-group insurance, the population it will release to the semi-group market will be especially rich in young, responsible low risks.

It is quite possible, if insurers behave rationally, that they will compete for this market by offering a relatively low-cost, preferred provider organization (PPO)–type product in a standardized form with only a few questions to determine premiums, such as age, family size, and employment type and status. Even some features that might otherwise be objectionable, such as time-limited preexisting-condition exclusions to discourage dropouts, could lead to a stable market with minimal premium variation.

Conclusion

Removing the tax subsidy would lead small employers, for whom group insurance has not been truly efficient, to drop coverage, raise wages, and steer employees toward other sources of insurance. The biggest threat to the establishment of a flexible, functioning insurance market in the absence of a differential tax might still be government itself. Too-heavy regulation of the content of coverage or of premium variation is likely to produce exactly the risk segmentation (through cream skimming) it seeks to avoid. The availability of charity or Medicaid will also crowd out the private market; this threat can be greatly attenuated by using the proceeds of the tax subsidy to provide predetermined, substantial tax credits toward obtaining private insurance, regardless of whether the market is employment-based, semi-group, or individual. Perfection cannot be attained, but improvement over the current state of affairs is surely possible.

6

❖

Conclusions and Implications

The topic of risk pooling and risk segmentation is undoubtedly the most complex, confusing, and contentious issue in the analysis of insurance markets. Public policy toward risk pooling and risk segmentation is probably the most difficult to formulate and implement in ways that avoid unintended consequences and do more good than harm.

The analysis and evidence presented in this study do not provide a complete picture of what happens or what could happen in markets, and they do not specify a can't-fail public policy or change in public policy. This topic is one that should always be approached with great humility. Nevertheless, they do perform some useful functions. First, they definitively disprove some common misconceptions about how insurance markets function. And second, they change the odds on what might be improvements in public policy, making some actions look less likely to provide benefit and increasing the chances that others will help. Given the present state of knowledge, no one can offer a sure counsel—and anyone who does so is sure to be wrong. We can build on these results, however, by outlining the key additional information that would provide the most help in policy formulation.

What Isn't Necessarily So

The conventional wisdom in insurance-market analysis assigns the highest marks for risk pooling to large-group insurance and the lowest to the nongroup individual market. Perhaps this ranking is correct, but our results suggest that the appearances that gave rise to it may be deceptive. If we look at what people actually pay and who actually buys this type of insurance, nongroup insurance appears to be much less effective in segmenting risks than one would assume simply by reviewing what insurers say they try to do. Considerable valid and good research, some quite recent, describes nongroup insurers who seek to charge low premiums to low risks and high premiums to high risks; to avoid selling to high risks; or to seek out low risks as prime customers. But this research is misleading, because it looks only at one side of the market—what sellers would like to have happen. If we look at buyers' objectives, most buyers (regardless of risk level) try to purchase decent insurance to protect themselves from financial ruin— and to do so at the lowest premium that they can find. (A small minority of potential buyers may not share this goal, of course. Low-income households may at some point view the acceptance of charity or bad-debt care as preferable to paying market-insurance premiums at average risk levels, which they cannot afford, to protect assets that they do not have.) Buyers appear to have some success in their quest for a decent deal, and they frequently choose policies with guaranteed renewability.

Our results show that there is much more risk pooling in nongroup insurance markets than is suggested by effective risk rating. Across a random sample of citizens, there is still substantial variation in the premiums paid for nongroup insurance for a given level of coverage—but that variation is by no means proportional to risk. We also find, in this small sample, no conclusive, statistical evidence to indicate that ordinary Americans seeking insurance in the nongroup market are differentially deterred from obtaining coverage because they are higher-than-average risks.

This nongroup market is, nevertheless, far from perfect: people at all risk levels are charged and pay premiums that are high relative to the benefits they will get back. High loading arises because this market, like all customized markets (and like its analogues in automobile and homeowners insurance), is very expensive to administer. The correct conclusion to be drawn is that the nongroup market is high in cost, though it may not be very unfair. Everyone overpays, and this discourages insurance purchasing with an approximately even hand.

What is to be concluded about the group insurance markets, especially the large-group markets idealized as "corporate socialism"? Here appearances are even less clear, and they are also quite deceptive. If we take the employee premiums actually charged and paid as our measure of what employees pay for group insurance, the picture is one of enormous variation—much more than for nongroup health insurance or for any other insurance. Some people take jobs where they literally pay nothing for insurance, and others pay a lot, although few pay the full per-person cost. These employee-premium payments do not vary with risk, but they do vary over a wide range. The odds that an employee will pay a premium two or three times the average under group insurance are much higher than the odds of similar discrimination in the nongroup market, although of course the absolute value of the average employee premium is lower than the average nongroup premium for the same coverage.

Economists will object to the preceding discussion because it ignores the bulk of the premium for employment-based coverage nominally paid by the employer. Of course, if the employer really does pay the premium by accepting lower profits or raising prices to consumers, these premiums are spread around, albeit in an uneven (and perhaps illogical) way. But virtually all economists believe that in some reasonably moderate run, the employer premium in the aggregate comes out of worker wages. Even if this proposition were granted (and not all policymakers would grant it), it leaves the difficult unanswered question: If employees sacrifice wages, *which* employees sacrifice *how much*? The data custodians at the Agency for Health Care Policy and Research assumed that this total charge comes out of wages on a uniform, per-employee basis, but their survey offers no evidence that this is so, and no enunciated basis in theory for concluding that it is likely to happen. Your guess is as good as theirs.

Although we will talk about some hints for better guessing presently, our firm conclusion is that no one really knows how this cost is distributed, and no one knows whether it might be related to risk or to something else that leads to substantial and unpredictable variation across individuals. After all, the problem is not that high risks pay premiums much above average, but that *anyone* pays premiums much above average, because of unforeseen events over which they have no control. Such created uncertainty is surely possible in the group market.

What Probably Is So

This study provides circumstantial evidence for an important conclusion already known from other sources. The serious problem with nongroup insurance is that it is expensive (relative to what the consumer gets) for *everyone*, regardless of risk level. Our measures of variation in total expenses, including out-of-pocket payments, attest to the lower likelihood of having coverage for people without access to employment-based settings—even for people with adequate income.

The other certain conclusion is that *all* insurance pools risk. In 1987, the specter of insurance so accurately risk-rated as to be pointless was not present—as it will not be present in any future setting. The great bulk of the variation in actual health expenses and benefits, our results clearly show, is always unpredictable. People who buy insurance and get sick receive transfers after the fact from people who buy insurance and do not get sick. Of course the latter group, unfortunate as it is to have been "taken" by the insurer in a financial sense, would surely not trade places with the former.

The most important policy implication from this discussion is that political energy should be directed toward designing ways to furnish good and cheap insurance, and should not be diverted into a fixation with risk segmentation. Indeed, influences other than risk cause so much apparent variation in total premiums for a given, nominal level of coverage that the variation attributable to risk levels is very difficult to detect, much less isolate. The possibility of risk segmentation may be the Achilles' heel of heroic competitive insurance markets, but this particular organism has many other, more immediately threatening points of vulnerability.

Getting a Grip

Both the theory and the empirical results in this study challenge the conventional wisdom on the comparative performance of different types of health insurance markets, some much beloved and others much reviled. Not only should challenges to what everyone thinks be made with caution, but more important, one or a few econometric studies (or one or a few data sets) cannot be taken as definitive. Since this type of evidence is necessarily circumstantial, we need a preponderance of it. So we wonder whether there are other explanations for what we have found and failed to find, and other data consistent or inconsistent with these messages.

As noted at several points in this study, there is no such thing as an objective measure of risk, and there are no data that would measure insurers' expectations of expenses for potential customers. (Such information exists in principle, but it would require a survey of under-writers, not a survey of consumers.) What we do examine are possible relationships among some of the objective measures that insurers use to estimate risk, on the one hand, and nongroup insurance premiums and purchases, on the other. While these measures do predict medical expenses and benefits, we could find no strong, consistent, and statistically significant relationships between these measures and premiums or purchasing.

These negative results are instructive, but there is a possibility that the data set, large as it initially was, is inadequate for a definitive test. The problem is simple: high-risk individuals (particularly those who are uninsured) are by definition relatively rare. Table 6–1 shows some evidence that bears on this matter. If we define high risk as the presence of a prior chronic condition in the under-sixty-five, noninstitutionalized population, we see that it is relatively common and uniformly distributed by employment or insurance arrangement across workers and their dependents. The effect of the presence of such a condition on expected expenses is large enough that some effect on premiums, if present, should have been detected. Conversely, if we define *high risk* as expected expense greater than 200 percent of the average (controlling for age, gender, and location), we see that this phenomenon is rather rare, although again fairly uniformly distributed. The conclusion is that if it takes this much of a boost in risk to affect premiums, either high risk happens so rarely as to be undetectable by our data or it has no relationship to premiums.

Toward a Big-Picture Policy

What do our results mean for the formulation of policy toward private health insurance in general and employment-based health insurance in particular? We have already commented at some length on tax policy. The theoretically important and empirically measured effects of the differential tax subsidy on employment-based health insurance are well known. The subsidy is inequitable, horizontally and vertically. It leads to excessive levels of insurance coverage—and to deficient levels of opportunities for individual choice of coverage—especially in small firms. Our results strongly suggest that the only good thing left to say about the tax subsidy—that it does, despite all these harms, strongly encourage risk pooling—is probably not true. Considerable pooling occurs even without the subsidy. It does not encourage much more pooling, and some of the redistribution it might sometimes encourage across risk classes—redistribution from young workers in large firms to middle-aged workers in large firms, but not across firms—is not especially socially desirable.

Above and beyond these old arguments, however, are there really better ways to provide health insurance than through the employment setting, and should the subsidization of that setting be stopped? We have already noted major advantages of such insurance: first, it leads to low administrative costs, and second, requiring payments of a large portion of the premium as a compulsory part of the employment contract causes people of uniform risk to retain coverage rather than to neglect it (as happens, on occasion, with other consumer insurances bought individually). This persistence also helps to keep administrative costs down.

There is a third possible advantage of group insurance, somewhat related to the others. It may well be that group insurance lowers the transactions cost not only for the insurer, but also for the purchaser. Although people who are high risks for reasons other than age do not appear to pay much higher premiums in the nongroup market and are as likely as others to obtain coverage, they may well have to search and scramble more to obtain a "good deal" on insurance. Partly this is because of the current composition of buyers in that market, which prompts insurers to be skeptical and to play hard to get. An influx of normal workers from small firms—which would most likely follow after termination of the tax subsidy—might help a great deal. Such a costly and gut-wrenching search process is to be avoided if possible.

If improvements are to occur, they must address the major issues surrounding nongroup insurance: high loading costs, lack of persistence in purchasing, and mistaken choices. Some adequate solution to the sales, billings, and collections tasks is necessary. There may be no obvious way to solve this problem completely, short of mandated purchase, but improvements may be possible.

Directing stronger subsidies to all insurances purchased by lower-income people would help both to reduce the extent of the uninsured and to solve some of the marketing-cost problem: when you have a "$2,000 off" coupon or voucher, you find the sellers; they do not have to find you. There may be some innovative administrative technologies involving banks or pension funds, which could also help to ensure continuous, low-cost coverage.

Like the nongroup market, the small-group market also needs

TABLE 6–1

PREVALENCE OF PREEXISTING CONDITIONS AND EXTREME EXPECTED EXPENSE, BY EMPLOYMENT AND INSURANCE-TYPE STATUS

Percentage of Individuals with at Least One Prior-Period Chronic Condition[a]

	All Individuals	Large-Group Policyholders	Small-Group Policyholders	Other Insureds[b]	The Uninsured
All individuals	33.3	41.8	40.1	25.9	33.3
Full-time workers	41.0	42.0	40.5	43.0	32.8
Dependents of workers[c]	15.8	n/a	n/a	14.7	17.2
No full-time worker in family	54.6	n/a	n/a	66.5	50.9

Percentage of Individuals with Expected Expense (Linear OLS Model, before 1987 Variables) at 200% of the Average (controlling for age, sex, and location)

	All Individuals	Large-Group Policyholders	Small-Group Policyholders	Other Insureds	The Uninsured
All individuals	4.5	4.7	6.6	3.6	5.6
Full-time workers	5.2	4.6	6.5	5.1	6.0
Dependents of workers	3.1	n/a	n/a	3.0	3.6
No full-time worker in family	6.0	n/a	n/a	5.1	6.9

Cell Percentage within Entire Sample (number of observations)

	All Individuals	Large-Group Policyholders	Small-Group Policyholders	Other Insureds	The Uninsured
All individuals	100.0 (N = 8,990)	32.1 (N = 2,594)	9.8 (N = 693)	45.9 (N = 3,650)	12.2 (N = 2,053)
Full-time workers	55.3 (N = 4,933)	30.2 (N = 2,486)	9.2 (N = 658)	10.0 (N = 824)	5.9 (N = 965)
Dependents of workers	35.5 (N = 3,128)	0.5 (N = 43)	0.3 (N = 21)	31.5 (N = 2,510)	3.2 (N = 554)
No full-time worker in family	9.2 (N = 929)	1.4 (N = 65)	0.3 (N = 14)	4.4 (N = 316)	3.1 (N = 534)

a. AHCPR's sample weights are used here to calculate these percentages. We reweight these weights, however, to account for missing premium data for a substantial portion of the insured Health Insurance Units in our final working samples.

b. Other Insureds includes dependents of group insurance and policyholders and dependents of nongroup insurance.

c. Dependents of full-time workers are defined as individuals not employed full-time in HIUs containing at least one full-time worker. Thus, for example, a wife of a full-time worker working full-time herself is instead considered only a full-time worker above.

SOURCE: 1987 NMES data.

some work, especially for low-wage groups. Redirecting the tax subsidy would do the most good here, but so would some imagination
directed at ways to lower administrative costs. An improved group-to-
individual conversion mechanism designed to tide people over when
the employer drops coverage might help as well.

Setting Priorities

We return to where we began. How serious is the problem of risk
segmentation in nongroup health insurance in the United States? Our
research and that of others suggest that the answer may well be, *not*
as serious as is commonly believed. The risks that do not get pooled,
such as age, may not really need to be pooled. While there are possibly some pockets of the kind of risk rating that combines serious illness with high premiums, these are rare. Guaranteed renewability is a
common policy feature.

In contrast, there are other problems with private health insurance so prominent that they cannot be ignored. High administrative
costs discourage some buyers, especially low-income ones. Subsidies
are hopelessly mistargeted and ineffective. The availability of free
care, in the face of high prices and minimal help, discourages the very
people who need insurance from buying it. Policy should focus on
where it can do the most good.

Notes

1. In calculating the coefficients of variation (CVs) for insured units, we use AHCPR's policyholder sample weights so that our statistics are nationally representative. For calculating CVs for all units—that is, for those who may be uninsured—we reweight the AHCPR Health Insurance Unit (HIU) sample weights to account for the missing premium data for many of the insured units. In this reweighting procedure, we also account for the differing (decreasing) frequency of missing data between the nongroup, small-group, and large-group units.

2. In a previous version of this study (Pauly 1998), we presented results slightly different from those presented here. That is because the AHCPR recently released revised premiums for employment-based policyholders. There was an error in their prior imputation of some premiums of firms that were self-insured. This error led to a few high-end outliers, which in turn increased our calculation of the coefficient of variation for premiums in the small- and large-group markets relative to the nongroup market.

3. The NMES identifies separately the presence of the following eleven chronic conditions: stroke, cancer, heart attack, gall bladder disease, high blood pressure, arteriosclerosis, rheumatism, emphysema, arthritis, diabetes, and heart disease. Using the NMES Medical Conditions File for that year's utilization of medical services, we determined whether or not each of the eleven chronic conditions was discovered during 1987. If it was not then discovered, it was coded as a "prior uncertain" variable; if it was then discovered, it was coded as a contemporaneous variable.

4. We noted earlier that values for self-reported health status and the measures of disability or functional limitations may be highly correlated with their (unknown to us) 1986 values. To test whether they "belong" with the prior-

period or contemporaneous variables, we estimated separate predicted expenses under both these assumptions and found that those *not* including these variables had higher elasticities and better fit in the nongroup premium regressions. This led to our classification of them as contemporaneous variables. More important than their label per se, it supports our argument that insurers do not systematically use such health conditions (actually observed by them or not) in determining their premiums.

5. Additionally, Section 106 of the IRS Code allows premiums for employee-purchased nongroup coverage to be excluded from taxable gross income if the employer reimburses the employee the amount of the premium (National Underwriter Company 1996, 218).

References

Agency for Health Care Policy and Research (AHCPR). 1991–1996. National Medical Expenditure Survey. Rockville, Md.

Arrow, K. 1963. "Uncertainty and the Welfare Economics of Medical Care." *American Economic Review* 53: 25–54.

Bandian, S., and L. Lewin. 1995. "Overview of Insurance Market Reforms: Theory and Practice." Paper presented at the Alpha Center Conference: The Rapidly Changing Insurance Market: Policy and Market Forces. Washington, D.C. (March).

Blumberg, L. J., and L. M. Nichols. 1995. "Health Insurance Market Reforms: What They Can and Cannot Do." Washington, D.C.: Urban Institute.

Browne, M. J. 1992. "Evidence of Adverse Selection in the Individual Health Insurance Market." *Journal of Risk and Insurance* 59 (March): 13–33.

Browne, M. J., and H. I. Doerpinghaus. 1993. "Information Asymmetries and Adverse Selection in the Market for Individual Medical Expense Insurance." *Journal of Risk and Insurance* 60 (June): 300–312.

Buchmueller, T. C. 1995. "Health Risk and Access to Employer-Provided Health Insurance." *Inquiry* 32 (Spring): 75–86.

Chollet, D. J., and A. M. Kirk. 1998. "Understanding Individual Health Insurance Markets." Kaiser Family Foundation Publication (March).

Cochrane, J. H. 1995. "Time-Consistent Health Insurance." *Journal of Political Economy* 103 (June): 445–73.

Congressional Research Service. 1988. *Costs and Effects of Extending Health Insurance Coverage.* Washington, D.C.: U.S. Government Printing Office.

Cutler, D. 1994. "Market Failure in Small Group Health Insurance." NBER Working Paper no. 4879 (October).

Cutler, D., and R. Zeckhauser. 1997. "Adverse Selection in Health Insurance." NBER Working Paper no. 6107 (July).

Duan, N. 1983. "Smearing Estimation: A Nonparametric Retransformation Method." *Journal of the American Statistical Association* 78 (September): 605–10.

Ehrlich, I., and G. Becker. 1972. "Market Insurance, Self-Insurance, and Self-Protection." *Journal of Political Economy* 80: 623–48.

Goldstein, G., and M. Pauly. 1976. "Group Health Insurance as a Local Public Good." *The Role of Health Insurance in the Health Services Sector*. Edited by R. Rosett. NBER.

Government Accounting Office. 1996. *Private Health Insurance: Millions Relying on Individual Market Face Cost and Coverage Trade-Offs*. HEHS-97–8 (November).

Gruber, J. 1994. "The Incidence of Mandated Maternity Benefits." *American Economic Review* 84 (June): 622–41.

Gruber, J., and B. C. Madrian. 1997. "Employment Separation and Health Insurance Coverage." *Journal of Public Economics* 66 (December): 349–82.

Gruber, J., and J. Poterba. 1994. "Tax Incentives and the Decision to Purchase Health Insurance: Evidence from the Self-Employed." *Quarterly Journal of Economics* 109 (August): 701–33.

Harrington, S. E., and G. R. Niehaus. 1999. *Risk Management and Insurance*. New York: Irwin/McGraw-Hill.

Institute of Medicine, Committee on Employer-Based Health Benefits. 1993. *Employment and Health Benefits: A Connection at Risk*. Edited by M. J. Field and H. T. Shapiro. Washington, D.C.: National Academy Press.

Kunreuther, H., and M. V. Pauly. 1985. "Market Equilibrium with Private Knowledge: An Insurance Example." *Journal of Public Economics* 26 (April): 269–88.

Lee, C., and D. Rogal. 1997. *Risk Adjustment in the Health Insurance Market*. Washington, D.C.: Alpha Center. (March).

Levy, H. 1998. "Who Pays for Health Insurance? Employee Contributions to Health Insurance Premiums." Princeton University Industrial Relations Section Working Paper no. 398 (March).

Light, D. W. 1992. "The Practice and Ethics of Risk-Rated Health Insurance." *Journal of the American Medical Association* 267: 2503–08.

Madrian, B. C. 1994. "Employment-based Health Insurance and Job Mobility: Is There Evidence of Job-Lock?" *Quarterly Journal of Economics* 109 (February): 27–54.

Manning, W. 1998. "The Logged Dependent Variable, Heteroscedasticity, and the Retransformation Problem." *Journal of Health Economics* 17 (June): 283–95.

Manning, W., J. Newhouse, N. Duan, E. Keeler, A. Leibowitz, and S. Marquis. 1987. "Health Insurance and the Demand for Medical Care." *American Economic Review* 77 (June): 251–77.

Merlis, M. 1999. "Public Subsidies and Private Markets: Coverage Expansion in the Current Insurance Market." Paper prepared for the Project on Incremental Health Reform, Institute for Health Policy Solutions. (February).

Monheit, A. C., L. M. Nichols, and T. M. Seldon. 1995/1996. "How Are the Net Health Benefits Distributed in the Employment-Related Insurance Market?" *Inquiry* 32 (Winter): 379–91.

Mullahy, J. 1998. "Much Ado about Two: Reconsidering Retransformation and the Two-Part Model in Health Econometrics." *Journal of Health Economics* 17 (June): 247–81.

National Underwriter Company. 1996. *Tax Facts 1*. Cincinnati.

Newhouse, J. 1996. "Reimbursing Health Plans and Health Providers: Efficiency in Production versus Selection." *Journal of Economic Literature* 34 (September): 1236–63.

Office of Technology Assessment. 1988. *AIDS and Health Insurance*. Washington, D.C.

Pauly, M. V. 1997. *Health Benefits at Work: An Economic and Political Analysis of Employment-Based Health Insurance*. Ann Arbor: University of Michigan Press.

———. 1998. "How Well Does Employment-based Insurance Pool Risk?" Paper presented at the Ninth Annual Health Economics Conference, Cornell University. June 27–29.

Pauly, M. V., P. Danzon, P. J. Feldstein, and J. Hoff. 1992. *Responsible National Health Insurance*. Washington D.C.: AEI Press.

Pauly, M. V., H. Kunreuther, and R. Hirth. 1995. "Guaranteed Renewability in Insurance." *Journal of Risk and Uncertainty* 10 (March): 143–56.

Pauly, M. V., H. Kunreuther, and P. Kleindorfer. 1986. "Regulation and Quality Competition in the U.S. Insurance Industry." *Economics of Insurance Regulation*. Edited by J. Finsinger and M. Pauly. New York: St. Martins Press.

Pauly, M. V., H. Kunreuther, and A. Nickel. 1998. "Guaranteed Renewability with Group Insurance." *Journal of Risk and Uncertainty* 16: 211–21.

Phelps, C. E. 1997. *Health Economics*. Reading, Mass.: Addison-Wesley.

Reinhardt, U. 1997. "Employment-Based Health Insurance, R.I.P." In *The Future U.S. Healthcare System: Who Will Care for the Poor and Uninsured?* Edited by S. Altman, U. Reinhardt, and A. Shields. Chicago: Health Administration Press, pp. 325–52.

Royalty, A. 1998. " A Discrete Choice Approach to Estimating Workers' Marginal Valuation of Fringe Benefits." Stanford University Working Paper no. 98–008 (May).

Sabota, L. A. 1999. "Does Title III of the Americans with Disabilities Act Regulate Insurance?" *University of Chicago Law Review* 66 (Winter): 243.

Sheils, J., and P. Hogan. 1999. "Cost of Tax-Exempt Health Benefits in 1998." *Health Affairs* 18: 176–81.

Sheiner, L. 1994. "Health Care Costs, Wages, and Aging: Assessing the Impact of Community Rating." Federal Reserve Board, December.

Wonnacott, R. J., and T. H. Wonnacott. 1979. *Econometrics*. 2d ed. New York: Wiley.

---- ❖ ----

About the Authors

Mark Pauly is the Bendheim Professor, the chairperson of the Department of Health Care Systems, and a professor in the Department of Public Policy and Management and the Department of Insurance and Risk Management, all at the Wharton School, University of Pennsylvania. He is also a professor of economics at the university. Among his many publications is *Health Benefits at Work: An Economic and Political Analysis of Employment-based Health Insurance* (1997).

Bradley Herring is a Ph.D. candidate at the Wharton School, Department of Health Care Systems. He is a coauthor, with Mark Pauly, of "An Efficient Employer Strategy for Dealing with Adverse Selection in Multiple-Plan Offerings: An MSA Example," to be published in a forthcoming issue of the *Journal of Health Economics*.

A NOTE ON THE BOOK

This book was edited by Cheryl Weissman
of the publications staff of the
American Enterprise Institute.
The text was set in Bodoni Book.
Coghill Composition Company
of Richmond, Virginia, set the type, and
Edwards Brothers of Lillington, North Carolina, printed
and bound the book, using permanent
acid-free paper.

The AEI PRESS is the publisher for the American Enterprise Institute for Public Policy Research, 1150 17th Street, N.W., Washington, D.C. 20036; *Christopher DeMuth,* publisher; *James Morris,* director; *Ann Petty,* editor; *Leigh Tripoli,* editor; *Cheryl Weissman,* editor; *Kenneth Krattenmaker,* art director and production manager; *Jean-Marie Navetta,* production assistant.